A Battler All My Life

Joyce McCartan
with Jill Christie

FOREWORD BY KATE KELLY

Fount

An Imprint of HarperCollins*Publishers*

Fount Paperbacks in an Imprint of
HarperCollins*Religious*
Part of HarperCollins*Publishers*
77–85 Fulham Palace Road, London W6 8JB

First published in Great Britain
in 1994 by Fount Paperbacks

1   3   5   7   9   10   8   6   4   2

A catalogue record for this book is
available from the British Library

0 00 627820–5

Typeset by Harper Phototypesetters Limited
Northampton, England
Printed and bound in Great Britain by
HarperCollinsManufacturing Glasgow

To Mena, who shared my vision,
to Kate, who is always there to give me support,
and to Theresa, who filled our lives with laughter and love.

Contents

Foreword 1

1 Beginnings 3

2 Escape to Bagot Street 17

3 The Terrors Begin 37

4 Family Feminism and the WIG 42

5 Gary 65

6 Battling On 77

7 America and Other Journeys 97

8 The Way Ahead 109

9 A Letter to My Grandchildren 127

Contents

Foreword

All of Joyce's waking moments in the midst of a chaotic, loving family life are spent 'studying': studying the next move in the battle to gain resources and improve the quality of life for those who live in her neighbourhood. When Joyce says 'I've been studying' it is a signal for those who know her to fade quickly or come out fighting. Hanging in there can bestow on the participants a mix of new energy, some frustration and great, great satisfaction.

The journey Joyce describes is her own, but it could be a metaphor for the journey so many women have made in Northern Ireland. Starting from a life governed by family and their immediate concerns, many women, especially in areas dominated by sectarian conflict, have begun their journey as enraged custodians of a better future for their children and their families. Like Joyce, they have played a pivotal role in identifying the problems of social and economic deprivation, and have often been the most courageous figures confronting sectarian conflict.

In their pursuit of a better future for their families, these women have found a new confidence in themselves. For the first time they have some control over their lives and have become an energetic force for seeking and demanding better provision of services at a local level. As Joyce illustrates in her story, their interests and energies are directed to all aspects of life in the community. The young, unemployed, elderly, handicapped, homeless, the environment are all part of their concern.

Professional boundaries and niceties are not part of the real experience of women's lives: they deal with the next problem, now, when it is relevant, just as they do in the normal run of their lives. Joyce's experience confirms this versatility, and her story also confirms the frustration of dealing with a system that is inflexible and does not reflect the dynamic, resilient life of a community at a local neighbourhood level.

Mornington and the Lamplighter on the Ormeau Road present the physical evidence of this contribution, which should be recognized as a vital part of the process of reconstruction and reconciliation in Northern Ireland. May they be just a beginning in terms of Joyce's achievement.

Kate Kelly

ONE

~

Beginnings

I've called my book *A Battler All My Life* because that, more than anything else, is what I've always been. So when it comes to describing myself as a child, I don't get the feeling that I'm talking about a different person from the one I am now. I haven't changed much at all. Very early on, I remember knowing that I'd need to fight and struggle for what I wanted. I also believed that if you kept on striving for something that was good, it would happen in the end. I don't know why I felt so strongly about these things so young, but one thing is sure, if I hadn't stayed the same, I wouldn't be writing this book; my life would have been so different.

I was born in 1929 in a lovely wee town called Banbridge – a very old place the other side of Dromore. There's a cut that goes up through the centre where the stage coaches used to go years back, stopping at the Downshire Arms Hotel, so it has history behind it. The house was low and whitewashed, with only one storey for all the main rooms, like the rest of the houses in our row. There was tar around the bottom of it and outside the front door stood a large barrel with a spout for the rain water to run into. You didn't have running water in those days in our street nor did you have electricity. A barrel which contained the cooking and washing water was handy being just outside the door, but for the drinking water you went down the long garden 200 or 300 yards and pumped the pump and filled your bucket.

There were two bedrooms. My father slept in one and my three brothers in the other. I was the youngest and the only girl and I slept in a small loft right up in the roof space, which I liked very much because it was all my own. I remember my bedroom being plain and wholesome with one small window right up at the peak of the roof. On the bed was a feather mattress that came up all around you when you lay on it, and that and the old-fashioned bolster were covered by a thick quilt. I loved that wee room. It was such a good place to escape to.

Some years ago the house was demolished so there's no trace of it left today. In fact, all the houses in the row got knocked down and it's hard to tell now where they stood.

I must say at once that the thing that affected me most in my whole life was my mother dying when I was only seven. She died quite suddenly, of a heart attack, and it made a huge difference to me. I can't remember much about my mum, only that she was a tall woman, taller than I am now, and she was warm. You felt safe with her, and she smelt so fresh and clean. She was not only a great homemaker, but a great baker and knitter. She filled the house with her activities, caring for everyone and doing all the work by hand, which was a good deal in those days.

On top of the ordinary things she made patchwork quilts, all different colours, from cutting up old bits of cloth. They were beautiful and so bright stitched together. To get one of those today you would pay over £100, or maybe more. She knitted wee woollen tops with skirts below them, like suits, and made petticoats crocheted all round the bottom that went down below your knees.

Then, all of a sudden she was gone, leaving a huge space in the household. I still have a picture in my mind of the hearse that came to carry my mother away, going off from our house with me running after it. One of my aunts caught me, took me in her arms and tried to comfort me.

After she died they found a whole lot of clothes she left for me, all stacked up in a wicker box. She must have seen ahead, or perhaps she'd gone to the doctor's with her heart problem and been warned. Whatever it was, she'd made provision and knitted socks for my father and my brothers as well, so that for years they didn't have to buy any new ones.

Being the only girl in the family, the whole responsibility for running the household immediately fell on my shoulders – the cooking and the cleaning and all the different things that needed doing. My father and brothers just took it for granted. Going back to those days, that was how it was. I was one who preferred roaming the fields to anything else, however. One night, I remember, I forgot to bake the bread. When I came in at 9.30 p.m., I had to make the bread and wait till it cooked before I was allowed to go to bed. I was only nine or ten then. But I wasn't harshly treated. My father was stern and strict and he'd not allow me out if I did wrong, but he wasn't bad.

There was always an awful lot to do, everything not being so handy then as it is now. If it was freezing outside, the pump used to freeze up and we used to pour boiling water over it to get it working again. We heated the house with an old-fashioned range. How I loathed it! Every week I'd have to blacken it, then use emery paper to give the iron running across it a shine. It had to gleam so that you could see your face in it, or I'd be in trouble. On the mantlepiece I can still remember the two friendly lions, old ones made of heavy china and coloured brown and yellow, and then the clock in the middle. There was the brass which had to be cleaned regularly along the mantlepiece and there was the old wooden kitchen table, which had to be scrubbed until the wood was white, for my father was always very meticulous. It was the same with the big yellow and red tiles that covered the whole floor downstairs. There was no such thing as lino or carpet in those days, or if there was, we didn't have any. I'm sure you'd pay a fortune for all that cleaning to be done now.

And then there was the washing. Oh, my goodness! Imagine the holes I made in the collars, I did them that hard. You used a tin bath and had a board with ridges in it which you put across the bath. You rubbed up and down, up and down with soap. There weren't so many different soap powders then. You used a bar of Sunlight and put it on thick.

But much worse than all the work was not having a mother at such a young age. I can look back and realize that now. You had nobody to turn to, with only men around, and nobody had time for you. One thing I learnt early in life was you've *got* to have time for people. It makes them feel important in themselves and it makes an awful big impact in their lives to feel worth something.

I was a real tomboy when I was a child and I was wild, so I got a great kick out of being in the fields around where we lived. It gave me the sort of freedom I never felt in the house. I used to love the way the hedgerows were bent over and the shady hollows, where you used to get a whole big clot of violets or primroses. They always smelt so clean. I don't think flowers smell the same as they used to, probably due to all the wrong treatment they get with artificial fertilizers and pesticides. My dad was a very good gardener, very knowledgeable, and he took great pride in growing carnations, and they *were* carnations then. The carnations you get these days, there's no smell from them. When it rained in our garden, the strong smell of carnations reached right up to the top of the house.

Jobs outside the home I didn't mind at all. Every Thursday I went off to fetch a big pail of buttermilk with two big blocks of butter floating on the top. It was gorgeous. I couldn't have got home with it quick enough. On the way I used to pass a family that lived at the end of the street who kept pigs. Every so often I heard the pigs squealing, and I'd cry my eyes out. Later you'd see them washing the blood away across the yard. It would give me the creeps.

I don't recall ever being ill, perhaps because we ate such good, fresh, organic food; soda bread just off the griddle and potato bread with plenty of country butter on it. A lot of what we ate came from the land: we used to go out picking lovely, fresh mushrooms. We went fishing a lot too, in the Corbette Lough and other places. Either I'd be on my own or with my brothers and my father. We either fished from the bank or set lines at night and got up early in the morning to fetch whatever we had caught. I loved fish, specially in those days when the environment wasn't destroyed and you knew what you were eating. We would light fires, too, and bake potatoes. Many a time I came home with a black face, wearing trousers and looking more like a wee lad, to be met by my strict aunts who would say, 'Why don't you be more ladylike?' We had a vegetable garden, too, out the back, where we grew potatoes, chives, cabbages, leeks, turnips, loads of different things. I've got to admit that if I weren't so busy in Belfast I'd prefer to live out in the countryside where I could go on growing all those good, healthy things.

I had a smooth-haired fox terrier, a greater hunter and a great pet. Twiggy we called him. I'd often take him out with me to lay the nets for rabbits. In those days, roast rabbit was another treat, but that was before myxomatosis. The natural things we ate certainly gave me a lasting interest in good food and enough enthusiasm to do some work recently investigating food additives and healthy diets.

Apart from roaming around the fields and fishing, I read a lot – all different things including Dickens and Robbie Burns, the poet. My father was a great bookworm. He'd been sent off to the school run by an aunt of his who was a headmistress. He lived with her away from his parents for some time and got a taste for good education. He came from a well-to-do family called Buchanan, who originated from Scotland and settled in Derry. His family thought he'd made a bad marriage, but by all accounts my mother was a lady. By the time I was born he had one of the best collections of books I've ever seen – I was quite sure it was one of the best in Ireland. Loads of poets were in that collection, though I can't remember exactly who they were now. Sad to say, the last time I saw those books was in my brother's house and the kids were drawing on them. That was one of the greatest hurts I can remember, seeing those things being wasted. Needless to say, my father would have been very angry.

My dad also used to save cigarette cards with beautiful pictures of flowers and birds. We mounted them in albums. I wish I knew what happened to all those albums as they seemed to me to be full of treasures. There wasn't much entertainment at home, only what you made yourself. There was no TV of course, but I'm not sorry about that, seeing the awful programmes that youngsters watch today. I did spend a lot of time on my own, although I don't remember feeling lonely. It wouldn't have suited me to be kept in, but it wasn't as dangerous for children to ramble about by themselves as it is now.

Perhaps rambling freely developed in me my unusual independence and outspokenness, because from the start I can remember getting told off for not holding my tongue. That's one bad habit I had and it hasn't changed. I always thought that if you were honest and told the truth nobody could come back at you. But I've had to learn that people don't always like the truth. They often won't thank you for it and it can even make them angry.

I don't know what made me so outspoken so young. My father didn't have a lot of influence on me as far as I can tell. He was a man who could not show his affection easily, and I needed affection. I think when my mother died something in him must have died too. He lived in his own separate world after that. I don't remember him going about much when I was growing up, though I do recall going on some good walks with him. He was a brilliant gardener and a scholar like my brothers, and he knew everything about plants – which were poisonous, which would heal a cut, what you could eat and what you could rub together to make a potion. I found the fact that he could make up medicines from plants very interesting, and it didn't just stop with curing people either. One day I remember being very proud of my dad when a wee dog belonging to some quite wealthy neighbours took sick and was dying. They brought him to Dad for advice. The vet said there was nothing to be done and he would die, but when my father heard this he was able to make up a rub for the dog, just by knowing what things to pick. Those people were overjoyed with the results.

My father had affection for one of his children, that was Hugh, but never really got close to the rest of us. He wouldn't have realized that what I was needing was a bit of affection instead of sternness. It might have helped him if I hadn't been so undiplomatic, always upsetting people. He didn't like the fact that I was well known for this habit in the neighbourhood and I remember getting into so much trouble from him for my behaviour. On one occasion it was about a woman who lived up our road who was always grumbling about other people. One day she was standing outside her house complaining loudly about an old woman who was her neighbour and I came out and said, 'Now you're talking about her and you shouldn't be.' I was only about nine at the time and very cheeky. My father was furious!

I got into trouble a lot at school, for the same reason that I was always sticking up for what I thought was right. One poor, wee girl I remember well. She was almost naked and bare, her clothes were that bad. One day the teacher was after making her hold out her hand to get slapped for something very small she'd done wrong, and there was me jumping up and down and shouting out, 'Don't be slapping her.' Teachers don't like that sort of interruption and this one was no exception. As a result I got a reputation for being wild there, too. Why do children get called wild when they only want to express themselves? I've always wondered about that.

School made me feel tied and smothered. That was another thing my father couldn't understand, especially as all my brothers were great scholars. Ernest, seven years older than I, was a real artist; Hugh, the middle boy, was a landscape gardener; and Sam, the eldest, went on to be an accountant. They all went to the Tech at night and pushed themselves. And there was I, so different. I was full of resentment and couldn't get away from school fast enough. This must have been hard on my father.

Two teachers did the best they could with me – Mr Johnson and Mrs Mawhaffey. Mrs Mawhaffey comes back to me clearly because she was very warm. She would put her arms around me and give me a wee hug. I felt good about that, knowing that she cared, but even she never managed to cut down the wildness in me. Looking back, it was more to do with rebellion at what I had to do in the house. It was just too much with school on top; women's work on a child's shoulders. If I hadn't had so much to do at home I think I might have taken up a different attitude at school.

During these difficult times I always had a strong faith. It had proved itself to me. Quite often, I would find myself saying, 'Please God. Please God.' No matter how bad things were, I still knew that if a thing was right, good always followed it. It's this same faith that gave me the vision I have in my life today; of making things better for other people, for myself and my grandchildren. Each time something is achieved, it is as if the faith and the vision have come together to produce something that is right. You may ask, 'How can you tell that it's right?' and I would answer, 'It's the ordinary people benefiting.'

As a child I didn't see much religious strife around me. When I did come across it I found it very difficult to understand. People who know me now will know that in the work I do I try very hard to be fair to both sides of the community – Catholics and Protestants. Bigotry is rife in Northern Ireland and I do my best to avoid it. But this openness, which I believe in so strongly, is not the result of family influence.

My father came from a Protestant background and, although he didn't talk about religion or discuss it much in the home, every twelfth July he'd play in what was called 'the band' and march. That was a great day for us. On the thirteenth July we went to Scarva to watch the battle between King Billy and King James. Only the Protestants went to this fight and the Catholics stayed at home, which made for a funny atmosphere in the streets. It felt as if people weren't trusting each other on that day and the day before; they weren't as close to each other as they were on all the other days of the year.

There'd be a big 'do' at Scarva, with stalls everywhere. You brought a picnic and there was Yellow Man to suck. King Billy and King James would be on big horses, one white and one brown, and they'd mount up in the middle of the field and push each other with long poles, looking like knights of old. It was always King James that fell off and King Billy who won. Very childish it was too. But we all clapped and yelled, which shows how stupid we were. For it's what comes out of things like that – the bitterness and the hate – that has led to so much more. On that day, Catholic people who were your neighbours didn't exist. I enjoyed it for the laugh I got out of it, but I never knew what lay behind it or that it was about keeping up the tradition of Protestantism and Orangeism.

Now that I've wised up I must add here that history is as badly taught now in Northern Ireland as it was then. Catholic schools tell one version and Protestant schools tell another. It's always been like this. None of them tell the true history. If they did, perhaps a lot of people would feel silly and youngsters would grow up a bit straighter. I personally don't believe in looking back over history, especially in the case of Northern Ireland. I prefer to look forward.

When my brother married a Catholic there was a huge kick up in the household. My father didn't like it when it was on his own doorstep and he was quite angry. A lot of my aunts and great aunts gave off about it too. But I'll tell you – it's been the best marriage out. They had a hard time in the beginning because, unlike nowadays, they couldn't go away and get married. But Sam and Kay went on with it and married, and despite having so much against them at the time, they've been happy for the last forty years.

Before he got married, Sam had left home to go to work in

Dundalk. I used to look forward greatly to his coming back for the weekend because he was always good to me, bringing sweets and wee gifts. One day, I'll never forget it, he brought me to the dressmaker to have a coat and hat made. I thought I was a film star in that coat and hat, I was so proud of myself all dressed up. To me it was better than £1,000, and I loved him for it.

I had a few things given to me at Christmas: a new pair of shoes always, maybe a nice jumper and skirt. It wasn't a time for getting to play with expensive new toys like it is now. My father bought the clothes and my two aunts, Hannah and Rebecca, gave me small things, sometimes fruit and chocolates on Christmas Day and sometimes brand new pennies. One year I remember being given a lovely string of pearls. I thought that was wonderful. That was an awfully big present then, they seemed like magic to me. When you look now at what youngsters expect from their parents and the way parents get themselves into debt, it's so silly. In a few weeks children get fed up with big expensive things. I think they appreciate something small and simple and get more enjoyment out of it in the long run.

Nothing special happened on my birthday – not even a card, and as far as I can remember there was never a party or other children around to play with. Maybe I was the kind of person who didn't make friends, preferring to roam the countryside. I took a great interest in flowers and birds. I used to love watching all the different kinds of birds, like the wee robin redbreast and the blue tit and the yellow tit; seeing them nesting in the hedgerow. From an early age I enjoyed seeing things grow. I'm sure that is why having such a big family was no problem to me, though I never stopped detesting doing a lot of work in the house.

Thinking back, I've done so much in my life since my childhood that a lot of it's got blocked out. But there's another incident that I can't really forget because it was so painful and it taught me a big lesson. I was in an orchard – alone as usual, rambling through it – and there was a gooseberry bush and what looked like a round ball made of paper lying in the middle of it. I was nosey so I pulled at it and I nearly got stung to death. Out streamed a mass of huge hornets and they tried to settle all over me. I ran and I beat them off as best I could – huge, black, noisy things they were – but the stings were terrible. Fortunately one of my aunts was at home when I reached there. She caught me and grabbed one of those balls of blue that you put in washing to make it look whiter, and she wet it in cold water and pressed it all over my body. It worked very well in helping to reduce the pain and the swellings. After that I never forgot that you can meddle too much in things you don't understand.

My two aunts came over sometimes to help out a bit and they were both alike, strict and very possessive. My brothers used to love boxing and body building with me alongside of them, stretching those expanding things and lifting weights. This was one of the things that shocked the aunts very much and they often tried to persuade my father to give me up to them, so that I could be brought up more like a girl. Luckily he wouldn't hear of it.

Of the rest of my family, Ernie went to England and we lost contact with him for a while. Hugh got married and never bothered to keep in touch. It's strange what effect losing the mother has on a family: ours split up and never really came together again. As for me taking after my brothers and adopting their sedate ways, I didn't.

What settled me down at times, and gave me a lot of things

to dream about, was talking to some of the old people in Banbridge and listening to the yarns and the stories they had to tell. You couldn't help but be fascinated. They're long dead now, but there was also a household with some young people in it who were called Gilchrist. They interested me a great deal because part of the family was in America. I heard so much about America from them that I used to think it must be wonderful and dreamt about going there. When I finally went (in 1990) I got the shock of my life because it was so different. It was more like going into outer space with all those tall buildings. The poverty was so bad it made me decide to do something about it – but that's another story for later.

When I reached fourteen it was time to leave school. By then, no matter what my father said about bettering myself, I wanted to do my own thing. I was too young to leave home and I certainly didn't want any more education, so I decided to go into a factory at Seaford that made cloth. I remember this wee woman trying to teach me to weave and the shuttle flying out all over the place. 'Keep your eye on that. Oh my goodness!' she said, 'you're destroying it.' So I was still getting into trouble because I had no patience for anything. The job lasted for two years, and very frustrating it was. I knew I'd had enough and would, I'm sure, have got the sack if I'd stayed longer.

One night I couldn't sleep and kept thinking, 'I'm smothered and everything I do is wrong.' I made up my mind then and there to save up a few shillings and get away. The only place I could think of was Belfast, so one morning I just ran away. I left nothing, no word, only a bit of paper on the mantlepiece saying 'I'm away'. My father would have stopped me if I'd have told him to his face what I was going to do. I packed a few clothes, let myself out of the house before it was hardly light and waited for a train at the station. By the time he found the note I would have arrived in Belfast.

I don't remember being particularly frightened, even though I hadn't been anywhere much before. I must have been too excited, thinking that at last all that I had inside me to do would be able to come out. But I was wrong about that. It wasn't to be until much later, when my family was almost reared up, that I was to find what I wanted to do and love doing. Only then, after so many years, would I have the chance to look around the community, see the women struggling and ask myself, 'Why should we accept so much hardship and unfairness? Why don't we speak up?'

TWO

എ

Escape to Bagot Street

I wasn't nervous at the thought of being in a big city all on my own because I'd always been something of a loner. But what did scare me was the thought of running out of money. I hadn't brought much, only what I'd managed to save from the last few weeks of work. So as soon as I got out of the train I started walking the streets, looking into shop windows for job advertisements. I came to a draper's and there was a notice asking for a girl to work behind the counter. I presented myself and they took me on, starting the next day. Then I found a cheap hotel for the first night, close by.

I did feel lonely and strange once I'd got into my room and put myself to bed. I thought about what I'd done, leaving my father, and I felt sad. It was guilt I felt too, because he was a great scholar, my dad, and he'd had high hopes for me. I couldn't help remembering the times he'd taken me round the garden and shown me all the different flowers. If he'd been more affectionate I might never have come to Belfast because I wouldn't have needed to escape so badly.

I only stayed that one night in the hotel. The next day one of the girls in the shop told me about a room available in a wee house close by and I took it. Once I was there, safe and sound, I thought I'd never be scared of anything again. Four or five weeks went by before I got in touch with my father. He came up and saw what I was doing and where I was living. When he'd seen I was all right, he accepted what I'd done, but I can't say that we kept up with each other much after that.

The draper's shop was quite dull, and I can't remember much about that period of my life. It just wasn't for me, being a salesperson, even though I got on well with the customers and a lot of them came back and asked me to serve them. I wasn't able to settle knowing there was something out there waiting for me that I just couldn't put my finger on.

In the evenings I didn't go out much. However one night I did, and a most important thing happened. My friend Celia, who was living in the same house, persuaded me to go to a dance hall with her. I didn't know a soul there, but all of a sudden a young man came up and asked me to dance. He had the most beautiful set of good, white teeth – they were what drew me to him first – and he was as brown as a berry. To this day he's still got all his own teeth, though he may not be such a good, tanned colour.

As we got to know each other, I learnt that Seamus was a Catholic. I didn't care at the time and I still don't. Religion is a very funny thing, not just in Northern Ireland. So many people go to the church or the chapel and when they come out, that's them finished. They think they've made their vows to God and that's them Christians. I feel quite differently about it. I feel you must 'do' your religion. For me, it's working with people, helping them, giving them the support they need and sharing whatever you have – that's my religion.

Seamus and I lived together for nine or ten years before getting married. I've hardly told anyone that, because in those days it was unusual and people didn't like it, but I just didn't feel like getting tied down at the time. I still seemed to be searching for some sort of freedom or perhaps a way of expressing myself.

During those years we lived at Bagot Street, just off the Ormeau Road – almost the same place where we live today. We had saved up £100 for the lease of a small terraced house, and I spent a lot of time working and building up a home. To begin with we only had a bed, six cups and a couple of chairs. By the time Malachy came along it was the happiest wee house. I was delighted to be having a baby at last, and at that point Seamus and I decided to get married. I didn't mind because it seemed like I was going to be tied to him anyway.

I well remember going into the hospital to have my first child, because it was the very first time I'd been inside one. A rum place it was too. The birth was difficult and I said to the doctor, 'I'm having no more babies.' She replied, 'Mrs McCartan, you'll be in here this time next year, sure you will.' 'I will not indeed,' I said, but for the next eight years I was. A year and a month later Elizabeth was born, then came Seamus (Jr), then Kathryn, right down to the eighth child, Gary, with Steven, Rosario and Martin in between.

Although it was hard work, the babies released a lot of what was inside me, taking up my energy and occupying my time. It was good to have a family so close, because one rears the other. There's more closeness between them when they're all growing up together. I really enjoyed having a big family and to me it's sad when people are not blessed with having children. They miss out.

Bagot Street was a great place to live. We were all very clannish there, large families getting it tough with the low wages and the unemployment. If one hadn't enough, the other had. Many's the night there were two or three families eating out of the same big tureen of soup. Sometimes half the street seemed to be getting meals out of that pot. Seamus was mending the cars then, but the work wasn't regular. We shared almost everything: baby clothes, food, even the Benefit. If someone got their 'brew' on a Tuesday and two or three other families were short, they'd lend it out. Then, when they got their 'brew' on the Friday, they'd repay it. If your neighbour wanted to go to the pictures with her husband for a night out, you'd watch their youngsters after they had put them to bed.

Bagot Street was like a real commune with so many great people you could get talking to. Mrs Keith and her husband were a fine couple with two grown-up children. When I came to live there I think mine was the first Catholic family in the area. The Keiths were Protestant but that made no difference at all to us or them. They were so good to me, so kind. They used to take one or two of my children away for the day with them, and when I was having my babies they were wonderful. My first two were born in hospital. Then the third one, Seamus (Jr), was due at home, but in the end they had to rush me away. When I had my fourth, the Keiths came down and did all my shopping for me, buying the Sunday loaf and all the other groceries. I never had to worry about that.

Mrs Lewis came down too. She was a good laugh if ever there was one. My Martin's a grown lad now, but when I was having him, she would come in to help big Seamus to wash and dress the other children in the morning. She came in the evening too, and Steven would be standing in the tub with his eyes so big and brown staring out at her. Mrs Lewis was bad with her nerves and used to near murder the kids, pulling them about and scrubbing them. But she had the heart of corn. There were no baths at the time and I used to have a big tin tub in the kitchen. Mrs Lewis filled it up and pulled the kids in. They would be running around that quick to get away from her, it's a wonder they didn't slip all over the place. Seamus used to be roaring with laughter at the sight of it all.

It never took us long getting over having the babies at home, a few days only. With all the other wee children around you just couldn't dilly-dally in bed. Most women had them at home. It was only if complications set in you'd have gone to hospital. There wasn't a year when some of us weren't pregnant, but nobody minded as far as I can remember. God doesn't give you a wee baby without sending something to feed it with. One mouth more doesn't make that much difference – that's how we thought. Nowadays people would be horrified having so many to care for. If you were having a baby then you went on and had it and loved it. But of course, it was not a question of birth control: you weren't supposed to use it. Anyway we all felt that children brought happiness into the home, everybody seemed to agree on this.

I must add that there was never anybody brought up for neglect, no matter how poor they were. It was taken for granted that you looked after your children. We hadn't much, but our children went out with their faces shining, their wee frocks spotless and ironed. We often went round the markets on a Friday to buy clothes, do them up and wash them. You'd have thought they were new. Saturday night was always bath night. After we'd got the children fed and watered and bathed, up to bed they would go. Then we'd lay out all their clothes ready for Sunday morning to go to chapel or church.

The doorsteps would get a good scrubbing, sometime on Saturday. Often we all used to be in a row on our hands and knees. Then there were the windows to clean. In the good weather on the late summer evenings we'd get the chairs out and sit and talk and yarn away. It was just as cosy in winter, when we'd do a lot of calling into one another's houses.

I just can't believe how things have changed. I think it must be that life's too fast now. They were the happiest days in Bagot

Street because your life was so full yet there was still time to enjoy it. There was so much around you: love and friendship, and nobody talked about anybody else. If we had anything to say about one another, we said it to that person's face and that was it, nobody took offence. It's not like that now and I'm sure that's why we didn't need any counselling in those days – we had each other. That is what is badly missed in Northern Ireland today. I remember neighbours being so close and they used to give one another such a lot of help.

My great friend was Alice. She lived right next door to me and had as many kids. One of them was a wee lad who was about the same age as my Gary, called Tony. He was a wild wee bugger and one time, I'll never forget it, the bin man had gone up their entry for to collect their bins. Well, one of Alice's bedrooms was over the entry and didn't Tony run to the window at that moment and pee directly down onto the bin man's head. It was a wonder Tony didn't get murdered, the bin man was that angry. Alice came running over to me in tears with her face bright red, crying, 'Joyce, what am I going to do with him?' Says I, 'What did he do?' 'He's after opening the window and peeing on the bin man,' she wept. I've laughed since and so has she, but then it wasn't so funny because she was so upset. But what a time we had, and what friendships!

Alice was a good laugh too, and she had her own way of doing things. One day she came over to me, a Monday morning it was, and she said, 'Now Joyce, I'm taking a hold of his suit and I'm going to pawn it as I've just bought a new pair of shoes for one of the children.' That was her husband's suit she was talking about, and she went her way down to the pawn shop and pawned it. That Monday night he came in and he was looking for his suit because he was off to the dogs. Up the stairs he went, but it wasn't there. So down he came, and when he heard what had happened to the suit he called her all the names of the day. He never let on to her, but the Saturday before he'd won on the horses and left all the money in the pocket of that suit. She gave off to him and said, 'You won that bet and you knew I hadn't much money.' We had to all muck in and lend Alice some money so that she could get the suit back. That's one thing I never did – pawn. See, Seamus always knocked out for me and he always managed to find a few bob. So Alice got the suit back and she caught her man too for having the big winner and not giving her a ha'penny!

It was wee things like that that made such a closeness in the community. On Sunday morning I always like a fry and my kids looked forward to it. You'd see me doing a dozen and a half eggs or maybe two dozen, bacon and a couple of pounds of sausages. When my young ones brought in their chums I used to have to count the heads and tails of so many, not to mention some more sniffing at the door saying, 'Doesn't Joyce's breakfast smell lovely.' Often they'd come in and get some too. But things were awful hard for everybody in the area. One particular day, though it wasn't all that unusual, there were about fourteen in our house: myself, a couple of women and their kids, and only some, of mine. I looked in my cupboard and all I had was a half a dozen eggs, one loaf and a bit of bacon. I was frying away in that pan and it looked awful big, saying to myself, 'Please God, the forty fishes and all, let it go round', and it did. They were filled up. I'll always remember that – how far things can go when you're sharing.

One time we nearly came unstuck. My children were young and all around me, Seamus was out of work for a while and I had an electric bill due. I was going to pay it that Thursday – Family Allowance was paid every Tuesday then – when the electricity man came to the door and it was only Monday. A big hefty man he was, I'm sure he stood about six feet, and he knocked on the door and said, 'I'm here to cut your electric off.' Just at that moment Seamus jumped down the stairs and he shouted, 'You put your foot over that doorstep and I'll cleave the head off you.' I got back behind Seamus and I pointed to my head and made a dreadful face, as much as to show that Seamus was a wee bit off. The electric man rushed away and it gave me time to pay the bill the next morning. We had so many different ways of getting by.

There used to be a family that lived over facing us – I can't give them their real name otherwise they'd be after suing me. We'll call them the Browns. There were three boys and a girl from about seven to eleven and the mum and dad. The dad was English and so was the mum, and both of them dressed like the back of your hand, real smart, he with his leather gloves and all. But in the house you couldn't believe it, they were sitting on orange boxes. Then one day they decided to get a phone in. We never heard tell of a phone in those days, never. But there was one window broken and the phone was just sitting there by it. If anybody wanted to use it they'd just put their hand through the broken window and phone when the family were all out.

That's only half of it. There was a tailor lived next door to the Browns, a lovely man he was and a great tailor. Every time he went to his cupboard he had to say to himself, 'I should have had more stuff in here, sugar and teabags and tins of food,' for things kept disappearing. He couldn't put his finger on what was happening. One night he was sitting down close to the cupboard with its door open and the next thing he saw was a small hand coming through a hole in the wall. Into his cupboard it came and took hold of some of his teabags and disappeared again. It was the Browns' youngsters. They were stealing.

But it wasn't all bad behaviour. I remember one year going down to Ballyhornan for a holiday where we stayed in a big hut close to the beach. Do you know how many kids I had with me? About seventeen of them, including seven of my own, and some of them were teenagers too. But everyone had a job to do. One had to carry the water, because we had a well there, one had to make the beds, one had to do the cleaning up . . . It was like Joyce's army. They were all kids from Bagot Street and it worked. I was all on my own with them during the day and then some of the mothers would come down at night or at the weekend. My own job was fetching the fresh milk, and I loved that. The worst thing that happened on that holiday was the chip pan going on fire, and someone threw water on it and even bigger flames shot up to the ceiling. The hut belonged either to the Air Force or the Army and it was let out very cheaply to big parties like us. Being close to the sea you could go swimming, and as it was the end of August we went off picking blackberries too. It was great. I don't remember a dull moment or a word of complaint, there was so much for everyone to busy themselves with.

There was always Christmas to prepare for and, though we hadn't much, we made the very best of it. One year, it was coming up to Christmas and a lot of people were unemployed in the area. We were trying to get the bits and pieces together for the kids which we had started a couple of months before. I hadn't thought about the Christmas dinner, and it was nearly Christmas day, when a man came to the door saying he had about forty odd turkeys for sale at a reasonable price. They surely must have fallen off the back of a lorry because when I asked him what each one cost, it was so low I nearly collapsed. But I said to myself, 'I've *got* to have a nice big turkey for Christmas.' So I asked him to come back in a wee while and I dashed over the road and told as many women as I could get hold of. The result was we all decided 'yes'. So we bunched up and put in a few bob each and bought the lot. But we must have left somebody out for the next thing we knew there was a policeman at my door. I had only one turkey in the house by then, the others being all round the area, and I shoved it quickly into the oven whilst they searched the whole house. A good thing there wasn't a woman with them or she'd have known where to look!

When we first got to Bagot Street you could drive in both ends and we were the street next to the main road. So to take a short cut a lot of cars used to come round Bagot Street and then round the other way. It was really bad so we blocked off one end ourselves and demanded that it should be made a one-way street. With nearly eighty children living there we couldn't do with all that traffic and we got what we wanted. That meant that in the summer days we could get chairs out and really enjoy ourselves. Maybe there'd be one baby in a pram and toddlers running around, and maybe one of us would go to fetch all the shopping to give the others a break to enjoy the sunshine.

It was on just such a day, when we were all sitting out – Gary was still a toddler so it must have been in 1979 – that we heard on the radio Maggie Thatcher was going to take the school milk away. The children used to get a half pint of milk a day free and this was going to be stopped. I was angry when I heard this, and me and the other mothers said, 'There are kids worse off than ours which won't be getting the milk, either.' And that meant some children wouldn't be getting any milk at all, which was an awful shame because it would have been good for them as they were growing up. All the women in the area got stirred up about it. You met them going to the baby club or just out and about, and as I got talking to them I found that they really wanted to listen.

It was at that point that I began to think this proposal, to take the school milk away, might be what it would take to release me and start me fighting for ourselves and our families. A group of us got together and decided to tell other women in the area about the principle of the thing. There was loads of milk at the time getting emptied into drains and lots of other good things getting destroyed because there was supposed to be too much of them. The more we all talked about this the angrier we got. We thought it should be flowing down the children's throats. So we went around saying that this was what was wrong with the world – so much was being destroyed and so much was being hoarded. We wanted to do something about the milk issue.

There were enough women stirred up about it to organize a march. By this time I was learning that I had a way with women. I could galvanize them, get them behind me and get them fighting for what they wanted. We all mucked in, literally going from door to door all over the area of the Ormeau Road, telling people what we were going to do, that we needed banners and as many people as possible, and what time we were starting off. That first time we had about seventy people, nearly all women with children in prams and the older ones walking alongside them. I can just picture myself now. There was only a year between Gary and Martin and I had a twin Tansad. There I was, in the front line, marching down the Ormeau Road, and all the women behind me with their banners. I couldn't believe it had come about through me and, honest to God, I have to admit that I'd done it because of being poor. It was need started me – my own and other people's. Without being poor, my life would never have been as full as it has been, so I've never regretted it.

That first march to reinstate the school milk didn't get us very far. We went to the City Hall and asked to see some councillors but we got turned away. We weren't going to give up, though. The following week a bright girl called Linda Edgerton had the idea of borrowing a couple of cows from a farmer she knew at Carryduff. This she did, and there were such big tits on them. The farmer came too, and he was as broad as he was tall. He was holding one cow and I was holding the other, pure white and lovely they were, and spick and span. Down the Ormeau Road we walked again, with all the people in the Ormeau Avenue offices leaning out through their windows looking at us. I'm sure they were saying, 'There go some idiots', but on we walked to the City Hall with the cows going along in front. Mrs Burns, who was a big, tall woman living further up the street from me, was there and she had a placard which said, 'Maggie Thatcher Milk Snatcher', and someone else went hanging onto another which asked, 'Has the Cow Jumped Over the Moon?' As we got to the door of the City Hall, one of the cows lifted it's tail, and you may guess what it did.

Four of us were let in, but you know what they're like in the City Hall. They had branded us as Republicans, although the biggest majority of the people around me certainly weren't that. They came from both sides of the community. We talked and talked once inside, but we got no further. So we had to turn tail, as you might say, and go home.

A few days later we decided to walk to Stormont. By this time there were about 200 of us and we were beginning to get some publicity. Again, the women were from both sides of the community, but when we got to the other side of the roadworks on the Newtownards Road, a big, big woman came out at us with a Union Jack waving, as much as to say, 'You're Republicans'. One of our women said, 'Well, what do our children drink? Is it water and air they drink? Don't they drink the same as yours?' and on we went.

When we'd made it to Stormont, there was a certain politician who came out to greet us on the steps. He believed in all that we said and he'd indicated that he wanted to better us. But he couldn't have been strong enough against the others for the next day in one of the hardline papers it said, 'If the good women of Bagot Street and McClure Street would buy three or four milking cows and put them on the disused railway, they would have plenty of milk for their children.' And this was supposed to be a serious suggestion!

As so often happens in Northern Ireland, we had been branded as representing only one side of the community and yet, in fact, we were ordinary people – working-class people who were fighting for the benefit of the whole. We never did get the milk back until two years after we'd demonstrated and then we didn't know why it was reinstated.

When I thought about this first battle, I knew I was doing no wrong and I knew I was trying to improve people's lifestyles. Milk doesn't seem much of an issue, but it is to the poorer people. Gradually I began to get angrier and angrier, and through that I began to see a lot of things that weren't right. For a start, I thought we should have been treated better and listened to, specially when at the centre of it was the growth of children.

One thing that gave me hope was looking round and seeing all those women active at last. I'd got them out of their houses and made them sit up and notice that something can be done.

All they needed was a push to make them start fighting for the things that are right. Women have great things to offer but so often they never get a chance to develop these and they don't have the courage to push themselves. I was cheeky, awful cheeky all my life. If women would work together at putting the things in the system right that are wrong, there would be such change!

Almost immediately after the milk demos came the raising of the bus fares. My goodness, the bus fares! The City Council always decided on the price of the bus tickets and they were putting them up sky high, including the children's fares. I had three children that had to use the buses to get to school. When I heard about it I started counting up and I said to myself, 'That will run me up about £4.50 a week.' Four pounds fifty was a great lot in those days. So I got talking to neighbours in Bagot Street and found out that they were feeling exactly the same – that they couldn't afford it either. Some of them maybe had four children going to school and unemployed husbands. My own husband was up and down with his work, never sure what cars would come in, but even if we'd had a load of money, I would have reacted the same because of seeing people worse off than me. So we got together in the street and decided to do something about it.

First, we sent letters from each one of us to the City Hall asking if we could have a meeting with the councillors. I got Linda Edgerton to write mine because she was good at it. We got an agreement and a date for a meeting. When we got up there, the question of raising the children's bus fares was put off. There was a lot of silly dilly-dallying which made us sit there on and on. About twenty of us women stayed, saying we wouldn't go until we got an answer – we just wouldn't budge. In the end, we got carried out, head and tail, and dumped on the doorstep.

The next day we held a meeting at my house and decided we'd boycott the buses. We would not have our children using them until the fares came down again. We got in touch with a few taxi men in order to pay them to take the children to school. You would have thought that would work out more expensive but in fact, it worked out at 10p per head. We shortened the journey by taking turns meeting the children from school and walking them down the road and taking them up to the taxis each morning. This carried on for about four weeks, when the councillors got around to agreeing to meet us again. The second time round it was much easier. As a result of this meeting a child's token was introduced. (You don't see those tokens around today. They were like round coins and the children's one was cheaper.) So the bus fares did come down and in all it only took about six weeks.

Luckily, the taxi drivers gave their support – there were over a hundred children involved. Even the bus men encouraged us because what we were doing would benefit their children too. They were badly off, the same as us.

The success of this battle gave us all a great uplift. It's a tremendous feeling when you win through and you make changes that you know are right. It matters a great deal to me to know that a family will find life a little bit easier because something I've tried to do has worked out.

By this time we women were getting known for kicking up and trying to get things changed. Out of the blue an offer came from the Community Relations to take us away for the odd day out. It had got around that many of us never got anywhere, for the Troubles were on and we were tied to our houses. They must have thought that if we had more freedom we'd quieten down! I was approached, so I asked for even more buses to be provided than we actually needed. The place was black with them – twelve in all, and we all mucked in and made a big pile of sandwiches and flasks of tea and away we went down to the seaside. That was good because some of the kids had never seen the sea before, and we all thoroughly enjoyed ourselves. It was so good in fact, that we decided to do it a wee bit more often. So every other fortnight we had a bus run on for to take us down to the shore, or anywhere just to have fun.

But the poor husbands were getting left out at home, and every time we'd come back in the evening after a lovely, long day away, one or other of them used to complain and say something like, 'Now, Joyce, I'm going to divorce her. Too many nights out.' And I used to say, 'It's about time women got out because they need a break, specially after being in the house all day and looking after the children.'

For as long as I can remember I've felt that women should have more freedom and choice to do what they want to do. I don't know what I would have done if I'd married a man who hadn't realized that there was something inside me that I had to get out. Seamus understood this and I've always felt blessed with a good man, for he allowed me to work it out for myself. If I wanted to fight for some cause that would benefit the home, he'd agree to it. I think he was a wee bit proud of what I was doing, too.

From being encouraged at home, and because of winning our point over the bus fares, I got enough confidence to look around and think. I began to see that whole systems in our society are wrong. I asked myself, 'Why do people hoard when they have too much whilst others are dying from having too little? Is it to keep prices up? Well, if it is, that's wrong. And why does money make that much difference? What did we do when there wasn't much money, I'd like to know? We bartered with things, isn't that right?'

The way I feel about those mountains of food stored away with so many people dying – it's not food that's scarce, it's justice. And when you think of so much good stuff being destroyed when it could go to people who need it, it just about makes you sick. I don't know about the economy or anything like that, but when you look at Black Wednesday, when all those billions of pounds were lost, it wouldn't have hurt us at all if we had lost it another way, feeding the starving in the world. And what's more, I believe it's the likes of us who know what it is to want who are the generous ones, not the people with money. It should be a matter of great guilt that more is not shared.

Something else I started to consider was the training of youngsters. There are thousands that slip through the net every year. To most of the people that are in charge of them, it's only a job that gives them money. They should be thinking more of the young ones they're supposed to be training. The trouble is that we ordinary people who aren't scholars are not consulted, when we know what we want for our families, for our children. We can see the failure in these schemes and where the training just isn't being carried out. And why is it being covered up? I know that if dedicated teachers, practical people who genuinely had the interests of the young at heart, went out of their way to develop whatever skills these youngsters had, something could be accomplished. There are loads of jobs that need doing out there. It's a fact that every person has a skill and something to give in this life – to give their lives for – but often they never get the chance to do it. In my opinion that's another reason why the training schemes need to be improved, not just to enable people to earn a living.

There's another side of our education that I don't agree with and that's the 11+ that is still running in our schools. It's nearly gone in England but it's rife here, and a very woeful system it is. If you look at the records you'll find that while Northern Ireland can boast of some fantastic successes from the Grammar schools, the Secondary Modern school results are a disgrace. Children are leaving school unable to do anything and without any ideas or ambition to improve themselves. But you'll never hear about them. There are so many scholars here, and only a fraction of children truanting, a percentage or two – that is what we're told. Bloody lies! I've seen them every day there in the road and down the railway line sniffing glue and mucking about. You don't hide facts like that, you bring them out into the open and see what you can do about them.

Of course, it's up to the parents to do a good job as well. Most of them try to do their best by their children, but to my mind children nowadays are not growing up the same as they used to. There's not enough time spent on them in the home. I'm not blaming this lack of time on women working. Whether you're working or not, you've *got* to find time. It makes an awful lot of difference to everyone to have some proper attention, and it would help children to change, too. These days, they don't seem to show much affection to their parents, but if they had that wee bit extra of love and caring they'd be softer. As it is, many youngsters come home from school and their mummy's either at work or busy in the house, and there they are, left sitting alone in front of the television watching violence.

Bagot Street was good because we joined our families together and shared hardship and joy, whatever came to us. I suppose the reason I loved living there so much stems back to when I was a girl. Then I needed a sister for company, but it wasn't to be, and missing one must have helped to make me unsettled and impatient. Having a family and friends made me much more contented.

The whole street got knocked down in the end because the houses were too old. They gave us new ones, but even before that things had begun to change. The Government said that they were going to put a ring road up through McClure Street. A lot of people had their houses bought so the rest wanted to sell theirs and get out. That was mostly what did it – that and hearing about the growing Troubles in other parts of the city.

It was sad seeing so many go when they should have sat there and stuck it out and supported one another. Some of the good neighbours moved out through fear, which they'd no cause for because we were too closely knit. Mostly, the Protestants were the ones that shifted, because a lot more Catholics were coming to live in the area. That made things worse, as it encouraged ghettos to form. It wasn't that the Government encouraged them – people chose the areas that they wanted to move to themselves – but nor did it discourage them. I think if everyone had just sat tight nothing could have touched our community. We were mixed and we were happy and nobody treated you any different, no matter what religion you were.

When I look right back, even though I had some difficult times when I was young, I think it was easier to grow up in those old-fashioned days. We talked more and read a lot, and we often had to think up our own entertainment. My dad was good at that. He'd play the mouth organ at home and the Jew's harp, and we used to sing and tell stories. People stayed in much more so we never had babysitters. But for all that, I don't remember a lot of them being bored. Now it's all rush and hurry, and most of the entertainment is automatic.

But even considering the troubles and frustrations of young people today, it does not explain or give me any real understanding of the next episode in my life. So many people affected and so many lives destroyed and ruined, I wonder even now if it has come to an end.

❧

THREE

The Terrors Begin

It was in 1971 that Jimmy was murdered. He was my young nephew. His mother had died – my sister-in-law, Marianne – having one of her babies and it was Seamus's sister and her husband who took on Jimmy and Lily to rear them. There were loads of kids left motherless by Marianne's death. Seamus's mother took another two on and they went to live with her whilst Jimmy and his sister were in Holywood in County Down. The rest were spread around the family and they mostly grew up and got married.

Jimmy chummed up with a wee Protestant lad who happened to get engaged. There was a stag party in a hotel in East Belfast before the marriage, and Jimmy was asked to celebrate too. That night he was hemmed in by Loyalists so that he couldn't get out of the hotel, and the people he knew could do nothing about it. They had him pointed out as a Catholic. He didn't know those people except the wee lad who was his Protestant friend.

Jimmy disappeared and was found the next morning. I remember Billy coming away at about half past seven at our door and crying out that wee Jimmy had been found murdered on Dee Street. They tied him by the feet to the rafters, they beat him with pick-axe handles, they cut his ears off and burnt him, tortured him. At the inquest the prosecutor said that after so much it must have been a relief for Jimmy getting the five bullets into his head. His was one of the first sectarian murders, and he wasn't involved in anything – he was only a Catholic.

There were a few brought up in court for the murder (that was the Romper Room Trial – one of the earliest trials of the Troubles), but they got off because there was not enough evidence. His friend took himself away to England, he was so afraid. Fear does so much to paralyse people. Jimmy was only nineteen, and he'd just begun to make out after a difficult start without a mother. He wouldn't even have thought of it happening because it hadn't happened before.

We were devastated when we imagined what Jimmy must have been through, as an innocent lad, hardly more than a child. He had burn marks on his body – cigarette burns. To this day I can't get my mind around it. I can't understand how one human being can hurt another like that. And it was only the first killing for us. Less than a couple of years later Seamus's brother, Noel, was walking his sister home when he, too, was in the wrong place at the wrong time. He was shot dead in the street for no reason we could ever discover. That was the youngest one in Seamus's huge family gone.

My mother-in-law never did get over the loss of her youngest son but even that was not the end of the terrors for her. A woman like Seamus's mother is very rare. She had twenty-one children, but so many of them died, leaving her with eleven. Despite having so many of her own, she never forgot her forty or so grandchildren. Every time one got christened she always bought the christening set, and very lovely and special it would have been. All the names, the ages and the likes and dislikes of each one were familiar to her, and of course, they all loved her for this.

What I remember so clearly about this lady, who really was a lady, is her complexion. She had the most beautiful pink and white skin. You couldn't imagine anything nicer. And she was so kind, I think she must have been a saint. Now, there are very few people you'd hear saying that about their mother-in-law! At the time of Noel's murder she would have been about sixty-seven, not a very ripe old age, but without a doubt the shock and the grief hastened her death.

Not only did Noel get killed, so violently and senselessly, but shortly afterwards his sister's husband received the same treatment. It was only about two weeks after Noel was shot that Lily's husband, Johnny Hamilton, came to our house saying he thought he was being followed. Lily had been so upset and disturbed by her brother's death that she'd gone into hospital at Purdysburn, so Johnny would have been on his own. I remember Seamus trying to persuade him to stay with us, but he was a shipyard worker, a tough kind of man. He said, 'Nobody's going to put me out of my house. I've got a right to be in my own home,' and off he went to have a couple of pints before bedtime.

We were away until late that Friday night. In fact, we didn't get back till the Saturday morning at 2.30 a.m. As we approached the house my heart sank. We couldn't believe our eyes, for it was all lit up, and you just knew something terrible must have happened. As we went through the door another brother of Seamus's met us and said, 'Johnny Hamilton's dead. They blew half his brains out in Spruce Street.' What words! He'd been so strong and full of life just hours before. I didn't know how to cope with the shock of it, coming so shortly after Noel's murder. My sister-in-law Lily had lost a husband and a brother in two weeks.

My mother-in-law's heart was broken by these events. She was, in any case, sick, suffering from gangrene in a toe which had developed after she'd stubbed it. She was in great pain and for all that to come on top, all the tragedies to come together, was too much for her. I was there when she died, and I looked at her, so uncomplaining, and said to myself, 'Why is it always the good people that seem to get so much suffering?' Her heart had been overflowing and she'd shared all she had, and there she was, dead, only about two months after we lost Noel and Johnny.

I still have Lily living with me, sixteen years after these traumatic events. She'd been in and out of Purdysburn. Then she took to drinking and drank up all the compensation money she received for Johnny. There'd been plenty of friends when she got the money but then, when the money went, they went too. She was admitted to Purdysburn again. One day, a sister of Seamus's went along to visit her and found her miserable and confused. She was that upset she came and told us, 'Lily's in the worst place possible and she shouldn't be there. You just go up and see.' So we were up like a lilt, as quick as lightning, and we saw how she looked. There was nothing else for it but to take her out immediately, and she's been with us ever since. But I've got to say that she isn't always sure what's going on about her. When you have so much on your plate coming at you all at once it can't help but shake you deeply. It breaks you down, so there isn't much between you and things you can't control. It did this to Lily and she's never recovered, and it did it to me.

Shortly after my mother-in-law died I got scared and nearly had a nervous breakdown. I kept my curtains closed in my house all day long. I locked my doors and sat in the dark. There was never a night when I didn't wake up thinking somebody was going to come in and take the rest of my family. I had nightmares and would jump in bed at the smallest sound. Each morning I'd just about manage to get the children off to school and then I'd hem myself in again entirely, drawing the curtains and locking the doors. It was a terrible feeling of being overwhelmed and I never knew anything like it before. My family didn't know how to take me because I'd always been the strongest, where a lot of them would depend on me. Now they knew something was seriously wrong. I could see them giving me a lot of affection, but I couldn't respond to it because of feeling dead inside. Very little attention did I give either to myself or to them.

This went on for several weeks until one day, quite out of the blue, Helen Campbell called to see me. Helen must be in her nineties now. Then she was nearly eighty, and she still rode a rickety bike with a basket on the front. She's what I'd call a real Christian – a doer, not a talker. I remember her knocking on the door and me undoing the bars, after first peeping through a crack in the curtain to see who it was. She came in and she said, 'Joyce, I'm bringing a bit of sunshine and love into your life; marigolds and honey and homemade bread,' and she gave me these lovely, wholesome things out of her basket. I looked at them and cried, and she gave me her hand. Helen made me a cup of tea, and at that moment I began to come out of the depression. I never looked back after that.

Helen wasn't a neighbour, she was an old friend and the first Quaker that I ever knew. When she said, 'I'm bringing sunshine and love into your life,' I said to myself, 'God has sent her.' She was so like an angel, come to me when I was sitting in the dark, so drab. But I have never forgotten how awful it was being all wrapped up in that sadness and fear. That is why today I feel so close to anybody that has a sickness like depression, or is bad with their nerves. Having been through it myself, I know how scary it can be.

∽

FOUR

Family Feminism
and the WIG

There was a great movement, a wonderful organization starting up just as I was recovering. It's funny the way things seem to happen in waves – either all bad or all good. Luckily, this particular good wave has never ceased. It meant an awful lot to me and I'm still involved with it to this day. What I'm referring to is the Belfast Women's Information Group.

If you mention the Belfast Women's Information Group you have to be talking about the work of one particular woman. She's the one who started it – not alone, but it was her inspiration – and she is still very much involved with the organization. Kate Kelly has done more for the women of Northern Ireland than any other person and she's never received the credit for it. That is why I have dedicated this book to her, I admire her so much.

Kate was a civil servant and comes from a pretty well-off family – not that money ever went to her head. She lives in the Malone Road, the swankiest part of Belfast, but she doesn't let that affect her head either. Through her father and mother, and from being a teacher at one time, Kate must have gained understanding of people in working-class areas. She noticed a whole lot of things that weren't fair for women and she tried to make life better for them through starting the Women's Information Group (WIG). It has been largely through her that we've managed to get as far as we have. By encouraging women to think for themselves, Kate has changed not only my life but hundreds of women's lives out there. She's very practical and steady, good at getting hold of useful information, and good at giving women the confidence and reassurance they need to get cracking.

I first met her in 1974. The rents had just been put up and as usual me and some others in the area went down to protest about the rises. We bumped into a few other women at the Housing Executive and were told that there was a meeting going to be held for women to voice their complaints and to gain information. And there was Kate. You'd have to meet her really to realize what kind of person she is. Then you would notice immediately her energy, and how she gives people the strength in themselves that they need to go ahead and do something. For example, when someone came up to her in that meeting and said, 'Kate, maybe we can do this, but maybe we can't', she said, 'Certainly you can do it.' You could see immediately how much better they felt. Since then I've noticed she's done this with so many women.

At the time, Kate had been working in Belfast with three social workers: Mathilde Stevenson, Kevin McLoughlin and Sheila Jane Mally. They all got the idea that women needed more say, and that if the right sort of change was to come about, women had to have a voice. So they advertized through playgroups, mothers and toddler groups, school meetings and the NSPCC; anywhere where women could be contacted. They were setting up an Information Group that would meet monthly.

They had the shock of their lives at the response they got. There had only been two meetings before I got caught up with the WIG and it wasn't long before I was going all over the city encouraging women to come along. I met with huge groups of women and I had so much success in galvanizing them that one woman was heard to say that if she were an MP she'd want me to be her canvasser. A while before I had tried to get a wee nursery opened in our area. It never worked out because we had no place for it, but it got me in touch with the NSPCC. This time I got loads of contacts through the same organization. As a result sometimes, even very early on, we would have as many as 400 women attending an Information Day.

The thing that puts you off most when you first start fighting for change is not knowing who to go to or how to go about it. From the very beginning Kate was always there with the sort of help any of us would need. You just had to lift the phone and ask for what you wanted to know, and it didn't matter how ignorant you were, she'd always be polite and nice. You might think that somebody like that wouldn't be bothered with people like us, but she was and she still is.

I've spent some time wondering how best to describe the WIG, and have come up with some good reasons why it's important to get the details right. Firstly, some readers, who aren't in Belfast and who want to bring about improvements, might want to organize similar groups wherever they are. Secondly, I owe a lot to the WIG and the support I've received from it over the years. Thirdly, the view that most people in the world have of Belfast is of a town beset with nothing but afflictions, and I want to put that right.

The WIG brings people together. It's not only the women of Belfast that cross communities to meet with each other regularly. We've run some exchanges – to Liverpool and London and other parts of Ireland – where women get a chance over several days to look at what is being set up in totally different circumstances. But having been to quite a few of these

I'd still say that the women of Belfast are the most active. Maybe it was the Troubles that made them get off their backsides to help themselves and their families, once they had seen that the Government just wasn't getting things done.

Basically, the WIG acts as an umbrella group to help women to start up things in their own communities which they see are needed. All the needs are different. Some women may want to set up an advice centre, others a mother and toddler group, or an action group to achieve something in their area. Some could be fighting to get a park for the children to play in or challenging the Housing Executive to improve a block of flats or review the rents – whatever is lacking in a particular area of town. The incentive is that you're fighting to improve your own district and any benefits will be felt directly.

In order to achieve your goals you have to have encouragement, know-how, contacts, and somewhere to meet from time to time. The WIG never had a base, until just recently – you just rang Kate Kelly, or Kathleen Feenan or me, whoever was taking the calls at their homes, and asked for the information you wanted or you left a message on the answering machine. If we didn't have an answer at our fingertips one of us would soon find out and pass it on in the next day or so.

Under the WIG umbrella we bring all the groups together once a month for a day of discussion, questions and answers. Before the Information Day comes up we hold a planning meeting to talk about what the topic is going to be. Kathleen Feenan, our Secretary, will have sent out invitations to up to twenty women in different areas of the town to come and help plan, so we get a good variety of ideas and interests to discuss. Maybe someone wants a speaker on violence in the home, or maybe education and how you can help your child; all different things like that. We sit and discuss what we'd like to hear about, all of us offering our ideas. Once we have decided, Kathleen will ring up someone she thinks should be good at giving us the advice we need and book them in.

To give one example, we recently had a professor from Queen's University talking about child abuse, together with three women from Women's Aid, and it was quite interesting. A lot of questions came up: How rife is it? What do you do to get help? Who do you phone immediately when you know a child is suffering abuse? After this we got more general questions from women planning to do things in their own area. Then everyone had a great lunch and a chance to chat more freely before being bused home again in time for the children coming back from school.

One very important job Kathleen does is organize the minibuses to pick up the women from all over Belfast. Without this, there's no way a woman with say, two small kids, could come. As it is, they know they'll be safely fetched and taken home again, and it makes a good day out for them too. The meeting is in a different location each time – we bus about like in America. So this month it could be Ballybeen, which is totally Protestant, and next month, Divis, which is totally Catholic. It doesn't matter where it is, so long as there's a big enough hall and room for a crèche beside it.

Each time a different group does the hosting and they also do the catering. The WIG meets the costs of each Information Day, and the hosting group will get a small amount, between £30 and £50, to cover their costs. Mary Leonard is the Treasurer. She's a good wee girl too, and an awful caring person, honest and serious. She comes to each Information Day; she has to, otherwise there'd be no money!

Another of Kathleen's jobs is to co-ordinate the work of the WIG. That means putting the new groups that are forming all

46

the time in touch with some of us old hands, so that we can give them a bit of a boost. I get called up very often by women who want to start up a wee business, or a drop-in centre, because it's in those areas that I now have plenty of experience.

One of the great difficulties, of course, is finding the funding for all this. It isn't difficult to get the initial payment for setting up a new, small venture in Belfast, but it's now almost impossible to get hold of the core funding in order to carry on. So you may begin by providing a badly needed amenity for the community, and it ends up you're having to try to run a business. We all believe that once a thing has proved that it's effective and of use in a part of the city that is downtrodden – whatever it is – the funding should be taken over by the Social Services or some other body because the needs of that area are being met. At the moment, core funding comes from private Trusts or government sources.

The most frustrating thing, and again we are in agreement about this, is that women are still on the outside when decisions are being made about policy. It is still men who make the decisions, and very often they don't have a great appreciation of what is needed. Where there's violence and a lot of insecurity in an area, it'swomen that are the most put upon, and yet they are the greatest support and the hardest workers trying to resolve the problems. It's women that can influence the children in the home and tell them, 'No! That's not right, I know better than that. I've met the people you're talking about, and they're just like us.' And women tell their men a thing or two as well, to put them a bit straighter. Through meeting people on both sides we find out we have the same problems. We can relate to one another on high unemployment, poverty, and worry over our kids, and together we can push to improve things.

One example of a success story which created real change and has managed to keep going is that of the Ligoneil group, and it happened as a result of watching and learning from other groups. The women of Ligoneil had attended the Information Days regularly. To begin with, they were meeting once a week in a church hall, paying £10 for it each time. The children were with them of course, but it was cold and draughty. We got a phone call one day for advice, and I told them to get their own place because then they could open and shut it when they liked; they'd be in charge and they could improve it to suit their needs. Eventually, with a lot of encouragement, they got hold of a house of their own. But they hadn't moved into it and we noticed one Information Day that they looked a bit depressed. So I rang them and invited them down for a cup of tea or coffee, and during the conversation my friend Mena found out what was wrong. It wasn't anything serious, like insurance or running costs or anything like that. Do you know what it was that was bothering them? They didn't know what to do because they hadn't a stove to cook on. There was a cooker out in our yard, as it happened. Kevin McLoughlin had helped them already with the negotiations for the house, and he got the stove lifted and brought up to them right away so they were into the house the next day. It was just that little bit of practical help they needed, and without it they could have got stuck.

There's another story which shows something more about the way women go about things. All of us got involved in this one, including Kate Kelly. Sometime in the 1980s the Government decided to pay out for the setting up of 'Family Centres' in Belfast – each one cost a quarter of a million pounds. They were called 'Family Centres' but they were really for mothers and children. There were separate rooms for 'consultations' and masses of space for staff to park their cars.

In fact, this was *social work*, and as everybody knows, if you put a label like that onto an organization it's likely to be avoided. As it happened, only special people 'in need of help' were to use them, and children who went there got teased and taunted by the others. So the rooms lay empty day after day.

At the most, these centres could cater for only ten women, and we kept thinking that for only £3,000 a year we could organize a centre where all the women and children of an area could use the facilities. We weren't saying that some special cases didn't need social work attention, but that you could do it much more sensitively and get to know individual needs much better if you started off by mixing everyone and catering for the whole.

Some of the women told us they were actually frightened of the new, expensive centres, so Kate Kelly and some others decided to make a video called *A Place of Our Own* to draw attention to the situation. Kate arranged for us to use the facilities at Queen's University. We got those for nothing by asking one of the lecturers, Liz MacShane, to join us. Liz organized a lot of help and also got hold of the cameras which, because we had no money, were essential.

It all went well and we decided that since Chris Patten was in Northern Ireland at the time we'd invite him to a showing. We sent off a letter to Chris Patten, but for ages we got no reply – I suppose it kept being put back, like so often happens. Then Kate asked me to ring his private office to see why we hadn't had an answer to our letter, and this I did. Immediately an arrangement was made for us to go and meet with Chris Patten the next day. Eight of us went up, with Kate being the official who was to accompany us.

Everything was very smartly laid out, with the Minister sitting in a semi-circle surrounded by all his secretaries. But the one facility we needed, a video machine, wasn't there. This meant that Kate had to dash off and get hers from home and fix it up right in front of him. It was just luck it worked, because Kate was in a great stew by this time. But all went well and he watched it. We were all there to make our points about the stupid way money was being spent, but after he'd seen it there was a silence, and then he said, 'How much money do you want?' Typical of women, we hadn't persuaded him to see it to ask for money at all. When we explained why we had made the video he said he was more in tune with what we were showing than with many of his official tasks. So some of us asked him why he didn't tell them to stop wasting this money, since he was the boss. He answered that he couldn't because it would be like turning a station around, with all the architects, planners, everyone geared to carry on. So that was that. Kate, as the spokeswoman, had to do a quick sum in her head to ask for some money, since the Minister was offering it. She blurted out, '£3,000 a year'. It was to go towards running the WIG, which was helping women to find their own meeting places, but it could just as well have been £10,000 – it would have been the same to him.

Of course, we were completely naïve in asking for so little because it didn't nearly cover our costs, nor does it today – even less. The point is, women so often don't know how to get what they want because, as Kate says, they haven't learnt to play the game that men have learnt through the ages. But why should they, if it's to become just as intimidating as men? In the popular feminist movement there are some women who will never be feminists in the way we are. To remain true to all you believe in, including your family, and yet be challenging the system the whole time, is something very difficult to achieve. That's why we call ourselves family feminists.

I'm often asked if I support the various peace initiatives that have taken place in Northern Ireland in the last few years, and what I think of them. Myself, I've never followed the kind of peace work that consists of holding rallies and making public speeches. I suppose it has its place, but it doesn't seem to me to be close enough to where the trouble really is. For example, most recently, some people came up from Dublin and tried to get support in Belfast for a new peace movement. Well, they put their foot in it in the first place. It was after the horror of the two youngsters killed by the IRA in Warrington that they got going. Many youngsters have been killed here too with plastic bullets, but when their mothers went to Dublin to a peace rally one time to drum up some support, they got pushed out of the crowd. That's wrong because if you're speaking out against violence and you're trying to bring peace, *everybody's* got to be included.

What I feel is so good about the WIG is that it brings people together at grass-roots level, ordinary working-class people, and builds up their trust. That's really what makes it unique. We trust one another and we can say what we like to one another without taking offence. From that basis you can start working together in the communities. I think another reason it works is that we're a crowd of women who are concerned about what is really happening in the world today – concerned about our families and our environment, those things that are right under our noses – and trying to make things easier. If I were to describe the women involved as 'soft' I don't mean they're easy targets. They can be tough trying to push things along, but they care a lot. Right now I can lift a telephone and I can go round every area in Belfast and I can get help for whoever has come to me and needs it. If there's sympathy needed, you get it; if you need advice, you get it. There are very few places that's happening.

51

What has helped to make women in Belfast so active is they don't depend on their local men in power. This is because they want to work for both sides. The people in power don't want to see everyone working together, achieving the things that count in life. It's always been the case in Northern Ireland that if those in power can split the working-class people, they do. If it were otherwise, this country would be one of the richest and one of the most beautiful wee countries in the world.

Right at this moment, there are at least seventy women's groups in the Belfast region alone, and they're increasing all the time. Most of those have grown out of the regular meetings organized through the WIG network. Recently we've felt the need to make use of a small office, with someone there to answer the phone. The phone contacts worked so well in the past that it wasn't necessary before, and that kept the costs down, too. Something we've benefited from since we began is keeping things simple and direct.

One of the groups, when it first started, had a very bossy woman amongst the new members who kept on talking about 'constitutions' and 'forming a committee'. I thought Kate knew what she was talking about when she told us how she felt like dying a death hearing this woman carrying on. She kept thinking, 'Oh my God, if they do that now they'll be doomed for ever and a day, because once you've got tied up with all that it's very hard to change.' Anyway, they didn't, they kept themselves more flexible and now they're thriving. Kate was wise to know that it needs a lot of thought and open-mindedness to set up a group, particularly when it looks as if you won't get the funding you need without all that committee nonsense.

Another thing that works well is to make the venues as cosy and comfortable as possible. Often the women will come from places that aren't like that at all, and it gives them a boost if there's a really welcoming atmosphere, warmth and something to eat and drink. Without that friendly, encouraging feel in the air, nobody comes out with what is really bothering them.

There are other times when people can let their hair down, not just the meetings. Once a year we hire a bus and we get outside of the City Hall – about thirty of us women from all different areas, backgrounds and religions – and off we go for a weekend away. Everybody's excited and looking forward to it for they know they'll have a few drinks and a singsong. They need it after living crammed up for maybe weeks and months in a house. We have workshops and other activities organized, but the great thing about it is that we have time, each one of us, to sit down and talk to other people. Sometimes each person gets their own room or else there'll be a dormitory. And the only thing you pay is £15, because there's a subsidy – and that's good for the whole weekend.

Some of the workshops I've attended at the away weekends are interesting and some are not. I always tease Kathleen about it, for she's all into 'health' and that kind of thing. I come back to her after a demo or a talk and I say, 'Yes, when we're talking about health, don't forget that the poor can't always afford to buy fresh fruit and wholemeal bread because it's dearer. When people get a decent wage and a decent standard of living I bet you they'll be healthier.' But then again, thinking about it, when I was being brought up I never had expensive food like steak. There was always plenty of porridge, good potatoes, buttermilk and potato bread, all home cooking and organically grown vegetables. Perhaps we've all got too much out of touch with the countryside, those of us who live in big towns like

Belfast, to be thinking properly about food.

The best place near at hand we've been so far is Benburb. I really enjoyed myself there. Benburb's an old place but I never noticed where it was because I got into the bus and chatted so much I didn't even see the scenery going past. On our time off I took myself away to see the old graveyard in the village. One of my favourite pastimes is looking at the old headstones and reading the words on them. I keep trying to picture the dead and whatever they were like in their day, and what sort of lifestyle they had.

There was a sister at Benburb, a nun called Sister Colette, and some time after we'd been there she wrote and told me she'd got her name changed to *Joyce*. She had to get permission from the Pope to do it, and it took ages, but it came through in the end and she was Sister Joyce Colette. She had told me she was leaving Benburb and going to England, where she didn't have to worry too much because she came from a rich family who would support her. The work she was doing at Benburb wasn't enough and she said she would have loved to be doing the same as me, and she envied me. I felt that here was a good woman who was a nun but she couldn't do what she wanted to do, and that seemed sad to me. It meant she'd so much to give, and there she was, confined. She must have felt stifled.

On the Sunday you were to go to church at Benburb, but I missed that. I always do. It was for a mixed congregation, and I was told they'd put on a sermon for both sides, but I felt even more that I didn't want to go, on hearing that. It's funny the way I feel about churches. Maybe it's because there are so many people that I see going to church and to chapel that disappoint me an awful lot.

I pray in my own time. I believe in prayers. Even when I'm walking about, going down stairs, I pray; more so on thanking and giving thanks to God for what I receive. Sometimes when you feel depressed, out of the blue something good can happen and you're saying to yourself, 'Oh, thank you God', and you feel so *different*. I feel God's all around, not just in churches or at any particular time. I depend a great lot on him, even though I'm not a church-goer, and he never lets me down. He *always* answers my prayers.

'Where is He?' you might ask. He's inside me. He comes from inside. It's the way you feel, the decisions you make and the way you lead your life that's important. That comes from inside, like your conscience, which is to do with God, too. If everybody would stop and listen to themselves quietly, listen to their consciences to find out the worth of what they're doing, it would be a far better world.

Another great trip we had went much further afield, all the way to Galway City, but first the Galway women came up to visit us. About fourteen of them came with another nun, Sister Frances, who had worked so hard to set up the Galway Women's Group. They went all about Belfast with Kathleen, visiting different places and exchanging views, but mostly the break was giving them a chance just to relax and talk to other women and get some information and ideas for themselves. We invited them up for a lovely lunch on Sunday and they asked us if we'd come down to Galway to spend some time with them. So we went, about eight of us, all women who knew each other well. We stayed in Sunshine House, which is kept for holidaymakers, and the Galway women stayed there too.

We had a couple of good meetings where we talked about our work in Belfast. The Galway women told us what a lot of trouble they were having with the high cost of school uniforms, and the fact that it was compulsory to buy them at the school outfitters. A story came out about one young mother who went downtown and bought her daughter's skirt and jumper for school, which were exactly the right colour but not the right shape. The clothes were highlighted in the classroom by the teacher for being all wrong, and the mother was angry about it and the child was embarrassed. Since I had had a similar experience when Gary and Martin started secondary school I fully understood how the family felt. We all agreed that we needed to work together to get things changed in that direction; that so long as the colours were right it shouldn't matter so much about the shape.

That night after the talks we went out and called in at a big bar right in the middle of Galway City. Now I would say there were about thirty of us. We were only in for about half an hour when Sister Frances was asked to leave. She has the most beautiful singing voice and she'd been singing along with the rest of us when we were all told to go. A nun barred from a pub! We couldn't get over it and we thought it was hilarious. It wasn't that we were drunk; it was that we were merry and they didn't seem to approve. I suppose it had never happened before! So we left and went back to the Sunshine House and had a wee party there.

There are certain nuns that don't wear a habit, they wear their ordinary clothes. They work right in the community, giving the women that wee bit of a lift and the support they need to do their own thing. Sister Frances is one of these and she's a very dear friend of mine, of all of us in fact. She's been our friend for the past seven years. I wish all the nuns were like her. She's jolly and you don't shock her. She understands that women who go away for the weekend need to enjoy themselves with a singsong and a wee drink, because it breaks the monotony of their lives.

The next day we decided to go down into Galway City to get a few bits and pieces to bring home to the children and grandchildren. We were just walking along the middle of the main street when all of a sudden there's 'Yoo-hoo! Yoo-hoo! Joyce, Janice'. We looked around in great surprise and discovered it was people that came into the chip shop in Belfast and were down in Galway working. Nothing would satisfy them but for us to go into a bar, so in we went. Some of the workers had won a big bet and drink was coming left, right and centre to celebrate, so we didn't get home until after seven o'clock. It happened that Sister Frances had told us the night before, 'The dinner will be ready at six o'clock. Now be in on time.' Of course we weren't, but Sister Frances had kept it all warm for us, which is so typical of her.

We were coming back to Belfast in the minibus and that evening down in Cork they had won the cup for the year playing Gaelic football. All you could hear going through the little towns and villages were cheers and yoo-hoos. Along the route we stopped at a hotel in a forest, where they had tables all set out on the grass, and there we had something to eat and another great laugh when we thought of being chucked out of the pub because a nun sang. Going home that night we were hoarse for having shouted so much.

Those weekends away organized by the WIG are, for some women, the only time they'll have of getting away from Belfast for a whole year.

When I first began going to the WIG meetings I was already clear about the sort of work I wanted to do. Through fighting for the milk to be put back into the schools and organizing the boycotting of the school buses to reduce the children's fare I had learnt an awful lot. What I had discovered about myself was that I had a strength, a gift if you like, for getting other women galvanized. I knew this was something very strong in me that I could do.

By that time I had also won a personal battle, where I had had to confront people high up in education. This was important to me because if you aren't a scholar yourself it's very difficult to get your voice listened to by those who are.

It happened when my two lads Gary and Martin were to go up to secondary school. I had bought them each the whole school uniform, which was compulsory, but when it came to a new pair of black leather shoes, I couldn't afford the £60 required. So instead I bought them each a pair of black track shoes. They went off to school with these on their feet and they were sent back home. Each day this happened, with them wearing the track shoes, and each day I sent them off again. For four weeks it carried on like this, with notes being sent to me saying my sons couldn't come to school unless they were wearing the correct shoes.

Eventually, they didn't come back home again. I thought everything had been sorted out and the shoes forgotten about, but in fact Gary and Martin were being put into a room all on their own just because their shoes were wrong. This went on for two weeks before the boys came out with it to me. Knowing that I'd be furious, they had kept it to themselves. But when I did hear I said everything. I gave off something chronic, told them at the school I should be taking them to court for not giving my children their proper education, and how dare they go about segregating youngsters like that. I took both boys out and picketed the building, causing a lot of embarrassment to everyone concerned. This sort of thing had apparently been happening to other children but their parents had done nothing.

I reminded myself that over the years the grandparents had

saved up to pay for that school. Every Sunday in the area they'd collected for that school to be built, but now the very children of the poorer areas who they'd saved for were being mistreated; those from the Markets area, the Lower Ormeau Road and the Short Strand, weren't wanted. 'Why?' I asked. I was so angry. So there was a kick up and for three mornings in a row myself and some other mothers stood outside the school drawing attention to it.

The priest in charge hasn't forgiven me to this day for doing that. I collared him and said there should be more people on the ground on the school committee. He started rhyming off: 'Oh, there is,' he said, 'There's myself, another priest, two nuns and two businessmen, Mrs McCartan.' And I said, 'So how would they have the understanding of families like us living down the Ormeau Road, trying to get by on low wages and high unemployment? Wouldn't you be better to have somebody on the committee more like ourselves, Father?' After that came a suggestion that we should go to the St Vincent de Paul. The St Vincent de Paul is a charity, and the idea was that they'd give me the money to buy the shoes. Now, I'm not particularly proud, but I thought it was an insult to tell us to go up there to get shoes for our children, and I refused to do it.

I just kept picketing and the result was we won the case. In the end the authorities said the children could wear whatever shoes they liked. I'm glad it happened like that for the fact that it highlighted the hardships of women who were badly-off. The grant towards the uniform was £30, and that only gets the blazer. If you have two or three children at school you have to look for shoes, shirts, jumpers, ties, everything – and the £10 charge for to register at the school. It's too often that these so-called 'small amounts' and requirements escape the attention of the better-off, but they're a matter of great importance to the poor, of great significance, and this should not be forgotten by those who are in a position of power.

The success over the shoes added to my confidence, and all in all I got the feeling it was time I branched out and set up something of my own. After I'd talked to other women and been to a lot of meetings I started to look around the area of the Lower Ormeau Road, where there's nothing much going on at all, for a room where we women could meet together. My great friend Mena Loughran came in with me. She also knew we needed somewhere which was ours, where we could sit down and work out some of our ideas and visions.

We had no money but I'd noticed that there was an empty building with a fish and chip shop downstairs and an office upstairs. I kept my eye on this and learnt that the man who owned both ran a pub next door. Mena and I marched into the pub one day and said to the man, 'Could we take that room that you have upstairs and we'll pay you whenever the money comes in?' To our surprise he replied, 'Certainly.' Then we approached Paul Sweeney of the Northern Ireland Voluntary Trust and told him we had no money but we had found a place for a drop-in centre. We applied for a grant but were told it would be four to six weeks before it would be through, so we advised the landlord that he'd get paid in due course and he agreed! It all happened like that, very quickly. Once you're sure about what you're doing, it often does.

We called our centre the Women's Information Drop-In Centre (WIDIC), and from the moment we opened I knew that this work suited me. When you have your own room you can open it when you like – at 3.00 a.m. if necessary – and you've got the space and the facilities to get on with things. There's nobody to interfere and you can use all your energy to start turning visions into realities.

Mena and I worked so well together even though our natures were very different. If anything went wrong and somebody needed some money, say they'd had a tragic death in the family, I'd say, 'Mena, we'll give to that person. We'll slip in a few bob; they'll be needing a bit extra.' Mena would say, 'Jesus, Joyce, we'll have nothing left.' 'Mena, God's good,' I'd tell her. 'Something always turns up.' And it did, often when we were least expecting it.

Through the WIG we sent round the information that we were up and open, and quite shortly we began to have groups of women – perhaps about fifteen or sixteen of them – coming in to ask us for advice. First of all they get a cup of tea and a fresh bap, and then they start talking about what they want to do. They'll come up with a whole load of excuses as to why they haven't set about it. So I'll say, 'What's keeping you back?' and I overrule their excuses with, 'Why don't you do this or that instead of sitting on your backsides?'

'Oh, we can't get a place.'

'Have you looked for one?'

'No.'

'Well, why haven't you?'

'It'll be too expensive.'

'Don't let money stand in your way,' says I. The conversation will go something like that. They don't always get going after the first meeting because they might need someone to give them more encouragement. I don't always have the time because I have to be in the WIDIC doing the work there. I sometimes wished there were a dozen of me keeping things going in those days. Even though I've got a full-time assistant now, and she's a wonderful wee worker, I still feel there's just too much to do.

As we got talking to the women who came up to the WIDIC

and they told us their problems we realized that there was even more unemployment and need in the area than we had thought. Our young ones were drinking too much and joyriding and getting into trouble because they had nothing to do but hang about street corners. There were loads of youngsters out there that had never been on a Youth Training Programme (YTP) and were roaming around bored. These were the ones that would get sucked into paramilitary organizations. Some of those that attended a training scheme found nothing in it to attract them, or maybe they attended for a couple of months where they'd be brushing floors and doing odd jobs with no point to them. The women were worried and didn't know what to do. What do you say to your son or daughter who sees no future? So at the same time as running the WIDIC we started to negotiate to buy the next door building to turn it into a local training centre, one that would not dodge the needs of our youngsters.

Not all that many people will have had the experience of living in a poor community without facilities in a town like Belfast. It would be difficult for those who haven't to imagine what a terrific boost it is when things start to pick up.

You may ask why I've concentrated on the Ormeau Road district for my work. The reason is, this is where I've always lived since I moved to Belfast forty-four years ago. It's also one of the most run-down areas you could find in the whole city, and for the last twenty-five years, since the Troubles began, it has been getting worse. Some of the statistics are a real eyeopener. We have 53 per cent of all employable adults unemployed. In the Ormeau Road, just the same as all over Belfast, people have been forced to leave their small businesses, the 'Troubles' have hit so hard. As a result, this area which was once thriving is now barren. As you may guess this makes the people who live here feel ignored and helpless, and loads of them live in fear for themselves and their families. The Lower Ormeau Road is typical of what's happening in other parts of the city, and before we set up the WIDIC and our other projects you could say there was almost nothing from one end of this strip of road to the other. Nothing that could benefit the people, hardly any shops and not even a tree to soften the whole thing, let alone a play area for the kids or a nice little restaurant for people to get out to in the evenings.

We wanted change, and for Mena and myself it was the busiest and happiest of times. We quickly had the WIDIC going smoothly and I loved the freedom it gave us to act. Listening to the women gave us a lot of insight and one of the things that came through was that some of their children were falling behind at school because they needed a bit of extra help with their homework. What children learn in school now is so different from what their parents learnt. For example, I can do maths my way and I can get the right answer, but if one of my kids wanted some help with their homework I'd never know how to go about showing them in the way the school wanted. This is a great problem and makes a lot of parents feel they haven't much to offer when it comes to furthering their children's education.

We decided to experiment by setting up homework classes at the WIDIC in the upstairs room. These classes were for the four to eighteen-year-olds – you couldn't have had a wider age range – and we asked twelve students from Queen's University and St Mary's Training College to come in as volunteers to tutor the children every Wednesday night. It turned out to be very successful, with twenty-four children coming in each week. Everybody gained: the students were getting valuable experience which would help them in the future to get jobs;

the children liked coming and their school work definitely improved. That year in our area we had four passes in the 11+, which was unheard of.

Not having enough space, with more and more work needing to be done in the office, we had to put a stop to those homework classes. We transferred them to St John Vianney Youth and Community Centre close by. The classes have fallen through recently due to a lack of resources. But if we get what we want in the end and can expand, we would certainly start them up again.

We also felt it would be a great idea to grow some of our own produce. So we had a couple of greenhouses set up on the back flat roof where space was going lost, high up so they would catch the sun. The idea was to supply salads for the workers' sandwiches at a cheap rate, and sell some plants. So we started putting in lettuce, tomatoes and scallions, and we grew flowers as well, mostly hyacinths for the tables. The second year we had such a crop of tomatoes the plants nearly fell over, so we lived off them for two months and gave loads of them away.

Sue Williams, a good friend to us and a Quaker, helped us a great deal in the early days. One day she brought down two cacti and before the end of the year we had hundreds of them; they'd all had wee babies, a dozen at a time. We repotted them and sold them at a cheap price, 15p each, so up and down the Ormeau Road you can see windows filled with them.

Everything was going fine, but my life never has run that smoothly or easily. It seems it's not for me to get along without having to cope with huge shocks and losses. This time was to be no exception.

FIVE

Gary

I usually had my babies at home but the night that Gary was born I went into difficulties, the same as happened with young Seamus, and they took me into hospital. It was to be a Caesarean operation, but before we even got there my wee last son had arrived in the ambulance. I was awfully ill then, but somehow that brings about a special closeness between mother and child. I was so glad that both of us were safe that I called him Gary Emmanuel, to say 'Thank you!'

When Gary was christened I noticed both his hands and his legs were jumping all the time – not that he was making them do that, it was happening of their own accord. I took him to the hospital and they did some tests and came out with the fact that because I'd never taken my vitamins when I was carrying him, he'd been born with too little calcium. I remember asking God to spare him and adding, 'I've called him after you.' Sure enough, Gary Emmanuel went up to hospital and they fed him with calcium through the head and he never looked back.

I need to say quite a lot about Gary before I describe what happened to him when he was just seventeen. If you don't know a person at all, whether they live or die is not of such great personal significance. It is from knowing them in all the ways that are just them and nobody else that the meaning comes in: the jokes they make, the sound of their voice, their likes and dislikes, what they plan to do with their lives. That's what makes them unique, though I've got to say that you don't always realize just what it is that makes them so special until they've gone.

I did feel a great bond with Gary, not only because he was the last child but because he was very like me. He was certainly always restless and hated being confined in school. Sometimes mothers get the blame for being in the wrong if their children fail at school, but I don't think I was at fault here. Gary used to truant and I had to walk him up to school every day to make sure he went. When I think of that now, it hurts me – school should be the happiest days of your life, but they certainly weren't for my son. He was too full of energy and found it hard to submit.

Right from the start Gary was a daredevil and he was fearless. He would try to jump off any height, and when he was only four or five he went up the back stairs of the big church near us and climbed out right onto the roof. I was washing up one day, standing in front of the sink by the kitchen window and I heard him calling from far off. When I looked up, there he was sitting right on top of the roof and waving. I nearly died of shock in case he fell, but he wasn't scared at all. One time he did fall off his bike and had to stay at home. He fretted being hemmed in like that and said, 'Oh, why did I have to break my leg? Why couldn't I have broke my two arms because now I can't get about.' He was delighted to miss school all the same.

Gary was very soft-hearted. When he left school he wasn't working and he didn't know what he should be doing. He'd done a year at the YTP and then he was back onto the streets again. So he and a young friend called Doc decided to take up window cleaning. They did it for a bit and then they came in one day with their monies in a jar and Gary said, 'Mammie, you know I've done the pensioners and I couldn't overcharge them, so I done those cheaper than I done the rest.' I always thank God there was that bit of kindness in him, and he thought for other people before he thought for himself. It's something I tried to pass on to my family when they were growing up, but you never know until you see it whether your influence has stuck.

I remember worrying about Gary a lot, knowing there was so much inside him that he needed to get out, but also that he didn't know how to go about it. Like me, he couldn't seem to express himself. I think that's what made me feel anxious – the pressure I felt inside him and the fact that he was fearless. He was full of fun and loved dressing up, but he never got the chance to do that sort of thing at school. I remember once we had an old dummy in our house that you could use for sewing. We had a nephew living with us and Gary dressed the dummy up one night; put a coat and a hat on it, and boots, and put it in his bed. Brian got a real shock – but that's the sort of thing Gary loved to do.

Then all of a sudden he started going out with Joanne. She was his school sweetheart and he began to settle down. One day he came to me and said, 'Mammie, Joanne is expecting a baby.' Well, I looked at him and I said to myself, 'My goodness, you're only a child yourself.' He was just going on to seventeen. 'You're too young to be a father,' I said to him. But then, they were meant for each other, there was no two ways about it. The only thing you could do was to give them the support they needed.

As it happened, typical of Gary, he'd fallen down a hole in the pavement at the back of the house some five years before and he'd received compensation. The money had been in the bank making interest all that time so they decided they had enough to start up and they'd get married in September. He went out and bought his suit and modelled it in front of me. I can still see him standing there and saying, 'Mammie, what do you think of it?' and looking so smart in all the new gear. They'd bought everything, all the clothes for Joanne too, and the two rings. When you think about it, sometimes it drives you crazy: so young and only just starting out in life.

It was one evening around eight o'clock, a few days after Gary had been showing me all his things, that I was in the Centre when I heard some terrible screams coming from the direction of my house up the road. I knew instantly that something had happened to one of my children, and that it was a daughter of mine screaming. I dropped the watering can and ran through into the street. It was Rosario who came hurtling into me, crying, 'Mammie, they've shot Gary.' It was such a shock I collapsed on the pavement. My legs wouldn't work at all and people came to give me water to bring me around.

They took me down to the house, which is only about 200 yards away, where my child was, but I couldn't go in to look at him. It was something I just couldn't bring myself to do. I learnt that Gary had been shot in the hall – he'd been combing his hair in front of the mirror just before going out – and that he'd run through to the kitchen and fallen into Seamus's arms. We all waited for the ambulance but I can't say where I was for that long time. It took twenty minutes to come and Gary was bleeding all the while. When they carried him out I couldn't look at him, it pained my heart so. I just kept fixing my mind on the thought that he wouldn't die.

Until very late we waited for news. None of us in the house could keep still and I had to get up and walk up and down, up and down. Then I saw the priest coming along the path and I knew. Until that moment I'd held out hope because they told me Gary hadn't been shot in the head or the heart, he'd been shot in the stomach. When the priest told me my wee Gary was dead it damned near killed me. Any mother who has lost a child will know what I'm trying to say; at the moment you hear, you don't know how to carry on.

I do remember getting down on my knees right then, knowing that I had to ask God to give me strength. He did, and he always does when you need it. I looked around me and I saw my family so stunned and shaken. Seamus had told me even before we knew Gary was dead that when he'd fallen into his arms he'd thought, 'I wish it was me that was shot and not Gary.'

What broke Seamus's heart, and mine as well, was learning the way Gary died. A wee nurse in the hospital was crying away, just after it happened, when Seamus approached her. She said a couple of seconds would have made all the difference: Gary bled to death waiting for the ambulance, with the hospital only five minutes away by car. Had it come earlier, there might have been a different story.

I knew it was vital that I made the right decisions: how to cope with Gary's murder, how to help all of my family to cope. So I prayed very hard for hatred not to enter my heart, knowing if it did I would destroy myself and my family. If hate's the one that has done the deed, you've got to stop it there. I went blank for some time; I had no feelings at all.

I got to know that the gunmen had entered the house looking for to shoot Seamus, but Gary had seen them first since he was nearest the front door. I said he was fearless – well, he'd thrown down a heavy, old hall stand with a wrought iron mirror in front of the two men to try to stop them getting any further. They didn't even have masks on. Kathryn, another daughter, saw them, as well as Rosario. They both described how the living room door was kicked open and the men sprayed the walls all round with bullets after they'd shot Gary.

You may ask why they were after big Seamus. There's no answer that we can find to this, but look how many innocent people are killed in Northern Ireland just because they are Catholic, or just because they're Protestant. About four months later the UFF made a statement to the effect that Gary was on the fringes of Republicanism, but that wasn't true at all. I challenged this publicly. Chris Moore came out to me from the BBC and I went on TV and told them that the only thing Gary ever joined was his hands in prayer. Not one of my family was involved or had anything to do with the paramilitaries.

Certainly some of my family were bitter against Protestants after Gary's death. Of course they'd had their arguments and their ups and downs as happens in every family, but if anyone did anything against one of them, they would forget their differences and at the first stop it would be each other they'd support. There was always a lot of love between them, and for that to happen to Gary caused them great hurt. I remember two of them saying 'I hate all Protestants' to each other, and I said, 'No!' and pointed out someone they knew who'd been kind to us. I made a point of telling them about the good people from both sides that came to visit me, sent me letters of sympathy and offered me their support. Loads of people did this and I couldn't have been more grateful. It helped an awful lot to know how many people cared and took the trouble to show it. I would ask my children, 'Do you hate so-and-so?' and mention a name, and they would invariably say, 'No, Mammie, but he/she's different.' So I would say, 'Well, how different?' I tried to show them that just because two people from one side had done this to their brother, it didn't follow that you hated everyone on that side.

Katrina, Gary's child, had been born three months before his murder. God was good to us in that line because we've all got part of Gary in her, living on, and she's the apple of all our eyes. Joanne has never got over losing Gary. He had been her first love and they got on famously.

The fact that nobody was convicted of the murder remains very hurtful to all my family. There was an attempt at identifying the murderers but, because the law says that a person has to be identified by two people and since only one of my daughters got a good look at the men, there was no case. The identification parade was a terrible ordeal for both of them. Seamus went with them, but even so they had to watch the man, that was later identified by one, shouting and fighting with the police before he was brought on. Rosario was able to do it, and the judge believed her at the trial, but Kathryn was too upset and came home weeping, saying, 'Mammie, I couldn't identify the one that murdered my brother.' Afterwards, two of my children suffered a lot of intimidation, being followed in the street and stared at where they worked. Both of them had to stay at home for several weeks. They'd risked their lives, but for nothing, because there was not enough evidence. It's that sort of thing that can make a very bitter pill to swallow.

It was in 1993/94, six years after this event, that we at the WIDIC produced the document called *Unfair Justice*, by which time we had seen plenty more examples of the law miscarrying. We sent this up to the Government as we believed it reflected the poor state of the judiciary here in Northern Ireland and most ordinary people's opinion of it. The gist of what we said was as follows:

Almost every day in Northern Ireland an innocent victim is subjected to the cruelty of others. Decent people everywhere are horrified by the news which hits the headlines, and only those who suffer can know of the horrors that no one else hears of. The question is: How can we stand back and watch this happening? How can we allow the terrorist to walk free from the court? How can we make the courts administer a just sentence?

The sad thing about our country is that our legal system seems to care more for the terrorist than for the victim. Who sets the laws, and why are they not responsible for the loopholes which allow these evil men to carry on with no suitable punishment?

It is time that our whole legal system was put under review. We put the law into the hands of one person, the Lord Chief Justice, who for all we know may be under the threat of the terrorist to reduce sentences. Some of the judicature are too old, senile, and bigoted! We need new, young fair-minded judges, who have no commitment to either flag. Those who are handing out the sentences are not beyond reproach for the leniency they allow to some, whilst others spend years in prison for the same crime. This iniquity has created division amongst decent and fair-minded people who have lost faith in this system. Once fairness can be seen to be exercised, then we can look at sorting out the 'Troubles' of Northern Ireland.

Each week on television we watch detectives in fictional programmes, solving the most intricate of crimes, and finding the perpetrator with scanty evidence. Fiction it is; unfortunately, this success does not spill over into real-life situations. There may be a lot of evidence, but our legal system disables the administration of justice. In the frequent instances when the perpetrator is caught red-handed in the act of committing an atrocity, he or she may have no fear of what is to come. A life sentence may only mean eleven years behind bars, or even six years, once the prisoner claims to 'have seen the light' – God works in mysterious ways. How can good behaviour allow a murderer any concessions, whilst the innocent victim is forced to face a life of suffering, misery, loneliness and terror? The terrorist has walked free from the court on several occasions due to a lack of evidence, despite the fact that there has been an eye witness at the scene of the crime, who has chosen him/her from the identity parade. These innocent witnesses live in fear, whilst the terrorist can sneer in the face of justice and walk free to commit the deed over again.

There should be one law for all, with a set of rules laid down which standardize the punishment. The judiciary should aim towards administering a greater punishment, rather than towards leniency.

We, as the public, should demand a reorganization and public inquiry of the judicial system. A more critical eye should look into the fairness of a punishment.

The Government, headed by what is supposed to be the party of law and order, must make sentences a real deterrent, with a sting of retribution. At present, there is no government representative responsible purely for terrorism, which is our greatest social evil, wrecking lives and deflating the profitability of our small, peripheral country. We demand of the Government new laws, a new judicature, and systematic equity.

I'm glad I didn't go to court in the case of Gary's murderers. Sometimes you have to block yourself off from a whole lot of things because otherwise they can haunt you for the rest of your life. Thank God I didn't see the face of the man who shot

Gary. But then again, I believe that as you sow, you reap. Even if the two that were there together that day aren't too bothered now by what they did, in later years they'll feel it.

I want to tell them, and all the others like them that are involved in violence, there's nothing so important that you need to kill for it – not a country, not a piece of land, not an idea. There's thousands here in Northern Ireland that have lost their husbands or their children. I'm luckier than many in that I have my work, and it keeps me going. When I see policemen and young soldiers on the TV with no arms or no legs I ask myself, 'How can one person do that to another?' I ask, 'What makes a person lift a gun to shoot another person dead, or leave a bomb that will blow people to bits?' This is not religious strife, it is thugism.

There are bad and good people on both sides, but until the big people with the power, both Catholics and Protestants, stand up together and work together, they'll not get rid of people like that. That includes the Churches, which are not, in my opinion, very honest. In Northern Ireland one Church is afraid of losing it's power to the other. Whereas, if they said they were all for God's people equally and turned their attention towards giving the support that is needed to improve the communities, I think there'd be an awful big change. I'd know then that Gary hadn't died for nothing. As things stand, I don't understand what he paid for with his life, or why.

The Christmas after he was murdered there was an essay competition at Gary's old school. One wee boy did it on Gary, the way he used to mend the bikes. Gary was very good with his hands, putting things together if the kids had punctures or anything, so they came to him to fix their bikes. He won the prize, that kid did.

About a year after Gary's death a parcel came through the post to the Centre, addressed to me. We all sat looking at it and were afraid to open it because we didn't know what it could be – a bomb perhaps? But we plucked up courage and I opened it. It was a wee book called *Opening Doors Within* by Eileen Caddy. All I know about the person who wrote the book is that she started a centre called Findhorn, in Scotland, where they grow a lot of their own stuff and it does very well. But, you know something, ever since I opened it and began to read it I've got real comfort out of that book, and I live my life day by day through it.

It seems the rest of the women in the Centre feel the same. The first time I read it out aloud, I've forgotten what page it was, but everything went still and you knew they wanted to hear. It was as quiet as quiet could be. Now every morning they say, 'Joyce, are you not going to read your wee book?' Not only that, when things are bad Janice and I will often open the book for that day and it will say exactly the right thing to cheer us up. Even the youngsters want to listen, which makes it even better. There's Eileen working with us, who's sixteen, who lost her dad in the killings over two years ago at the betting shop over the road – and a very decent and harmless man he was. Eileen will come over to me if I've forgotten to read that day and ask me to. I still don't know who sent it to me, but there again maybe whoever it was will read my book and they'll know how much help it has brought us all, over in Belfast.

It makes real sense with everybody listening, and I think what you get out of it is guidance from within. You stop and think before you do anything because you are always asking your conscience if you're doing the right thing. This in its turn changes you and makes you a whole different person. Where you feel warmth towards people, you care about them and you try to see what you're doing more clearly. It helps you to lead a life that's a real Christian life, where instead of kneeling in prayer you're doing what you would be saying in your prayers. And when things look up and turn out good you feel as if you're going to burst inside. You're near crying and you're saying, 'Thank God, Thank God', your heart's so full. The cover is so well worn and the cloth is all falling off on the outside for having been read every day, going into five years.

As this is Gary's chapter I'll end it with the reading for his birthday, 15 July:

You can help to bring down my heaven on earth when you realize that I am leading you and showing you the way. You will find all the directions deep within you, so you cannot possibly be led astray or take the wrong route. Seek within and follow those directions, and behold wonder upon wonder come about. There can never be a dull moment when I am guiding and directing you. Seek me and find me at all times. You do not have to look very far; I am there in the very midst of you, but you have to be consciously aware of me. As you live and move and have your being in me, you are creating the new heaven and new earth. There is no strain in creation. I said, 'Let there be Light,' and there was Light. I say, 'Behold my new heaven and new earth.' Therefore behold it, give eternal thanks for it, and dwell in it in perfect love, peace and harmony now.

Battling On

A short while after Gary's death I was asked to appear on television to speak about it, and I also spoke on the radio. I don't know how I did this or exactly what I said, I was feeling so numb still, but a journalist was kind enough to write about me in the local newspaper. This is what she said:

'Because I have other sons'

THE WOMEN'S Drop-In Centre on the Ormeau Road is part of Joyce McCartan's life.

She was there that morning last spring when the bare rooms above a fish and chip shop were officially declared open.

She was there when the women of the Lower Ormeau area worked to transform those rooms into a homely, friendly meeting place.

She was always there when anyone came with a problem or just looking for a sympathetic ear.

And she was there on that evening earlier this month when she heard the shots ring out that took the life of her youngest son, Gary.

Last week Joyce was back in the centre again, organising a Press conference for tomorrow morning, sorting out a problem with somebody else's knitting pattern, wondering if she should leave the tidying up to later.

Same old Joyce.

Except that she isn't just the same old Joyce any more. The shadows under her eyes are etched more deeply. Her grief and that fragility of the newly-bereaved seem to cling

---

to her. She laughs when others recall stories about Gary, the comedian of the family, but can't find the words to tell the story herself. She turns away with a smile on her lips and the pain in her eyes.

CRYING

When Gary was killed, the victim it is believed of a random sectarian shooting, the McCartan house just a few yards further down the Ormeau Road, was inundated with messages of sympathy and support from the women Joyce has come in contact with through the Women's Information Groups.

"That gave me the strength and determination to go on," she says softly.

She says that she still believes "there are so many good people in this wee country." She talks about the need for understanding and co-operation against the common evils of poverty, bad housing, unemployment.

And when you ask her how she has the heart to go on fighting for this understanding after what happened to her son, she leans forward in her determination.

"Because I have other sons..."

"And God knows whose son will be next. All life is sacred. When a policeman or soldier is killed, he's not 'just a policeman.' He's somebody's son. After Gary was killed, three policemen's widows phoned me to sympathise. It was terrible, terrible.

"They were crying down the phone. Some of those policemen had been blown up and the coffins had to be kept closed. Their wives didn't even get to see their bodies. At least I got to see my son."

Lindy McDowell
The Belfast Telegraph,
Monday, 1 June 1987.
Used by permission of
Jim Gray.

At the same time, so many people from all walks of life wrote me really lovely letters. Here are just a few to show how good they were:

Dear Joyce,

This is from a Protestant father of teenage daughters who has not written too many letters in his life (41 yrs). After hearing you speak on the radio about the tragic loss of your youngest son, Gary, at the hands of cruel, cowardly, faceless barbarians, I felt compelled to write to you and your husband, Seamus, to express my sincere heart-felt sympathy, and to send this small donation for Gary's wee baby Katrina.

I did not know Gary but I grew up on the lower Ormeau and knew his father Seamus. I was lucky because I was able to move my family out of Belfast to the country about 10 years ago, even though my eldest girl (19) has moved back to the city and lives in a flat not far from Ormeau Road.

What I really wanted to say is how much I admire your courage; while there are still folk on this little island of ours with hearts as big as yours then I believe there is still some hope for the rest of us!

For like you, I and 99 per cent of the people I know, just want to live in peace and raise our kids.

I won't say "I know how you feel", because no one except those poor mothers who have suffered the loss of a child, really know how you feel.

I will pray that God will give you strength for the long days and nights ahead, and also strength to carry on with the great work you are doing in the community, building bridges of peace.

These destroyers of life, on both sides, CANNOT win,

while women like you Joyce McCartan still live amongst us! Pity us men haven't the same "guts".

God Bless you and yours,
from A PROTESTANT WELLWISHER

Dear Joyce and Seamus,
I am just writing to say how deeply sorry we all are about Gary's death. I can't believe he is dead, every time I try to think about it, it does not seem true. I know how you must feel losing a young happy son like him. He was a good friend and I won't forget him in a hurry. I feel sorry for Joanne too after getting so excited about the wedding and now he's gone for ever. I bet he was so happy about the baby as well. I have enclosed a poem for Gary in the letter and, if you can, will you put it in his hand in the coffin? Thank you!

Lots of Love
Allison
XXX

P.S. Give everyone my love

Dear Mr & Mrs McCartan,

Just a short note to say how sorry we are for you and your family on your recent bereavement. Our hearts went out to you as we watched and listened to you on television.

Please try not to feel disheartened. We feel that if we ask our God to intervene and do as you are doing in building bridges and making friends, surely we shall see peace.

Our prayers are with you and may God bless you and your family in these difficult times.

A Police family.

They touched me very deeply and I felt, with so much sharing how can the world be such a bad place? My dear friend Mena Loughran was with me morning, noon and night at that time. She could see I wasn't too well all round because whenever I went home I couldn't get out again, and I took a bit of nerve sickness, like the time before when we'd lost so many of our family. Fear can do so much, and fear and depression together can near destroy you.

I thought a lot about Northern Ireland and the divided state of our country. It seemed to me that neither side could see the faults in our society for so much focusing on the Orange and the Green. And what is wrong with our politicians? I wondered. When they see so many people getting murdered and blown up every day and every week, they're squabbling over petty things: who's going to get the power? who's not going to get the power? Do they not realize that no matter whether we're Catholics or Protestants we are human beings and we're on this world for a short time for to try and rear our families, so why can't they concentrate on making it better for all of us? Why not let us have a bit of peace and stability so that we can have some happiness?

When you look around the homes in Northern Ireland and in England too, where people are missing because they've been killed, whether they're wee soldiers or ordinary people, there's the same sadness. I'm sure the English mothers think that the mothers over here are terrible. I feel for them too, because when you've been through it you can understand.

Many of the thoughts I had after Gary's murder I still have, but when sadness comes into your life, and tragedy, you don't go down, you rise above it. You ask yourself, 'Why do things like this happen?' and you look to see if you can make changes so that it doesn't happen again. You do things to stop it. You have to keep your hopes up and keep working towards betterment and then it'll start to snowball. I do believe this. I believe that having faith in things and making sure they're good, makes them happen. That's why I'll never give up and I'll never be beat.

So often I've sat in my office waiting for a group who've made an appointment to get some advice and in they'll come, and one person will say, 'Come on now Joyce, we've come to see what you're doing.' The next time you'll see them they'll be different - full of ideas and excitement, and they'll have seen all round and know what can be done. It's a wonderful feeling, to see people lifted. To me that's worth everything.

ᔕ

It was just as well there was so much to do after Gary's death. The fish and chip shop below the WIDIC luckily didn't last long because it was rundown and terrible looking, very depressing. Shortly after it closed we decided that it would be a great idea to take that over, too, and improve it, though as it turned out we were paying rent for about a year before we got off the ground with it.

We'd a great day when we opened the Lamplighter Fish and Chip Restaurant. We prepared for it for two whole days before. Everything was just right, all spick and span, when the fat didn't arrive! It is near impossible to open a fish and chip cafe without fat to fry in – everything rearing to go but nothing to put in the pan.

Unfortunately, someone who'd helped us and encouraged us a great deal was not able to come – Richard Needham. He rang through himself to say he couldn't make it, and think what I gave him for not being there! When I first met Richard Needham we had been waiting for a year for money to come in that we'd been promised for the refurbishment of the chip shop, from LEDU. We were finding it hard and I was worried. So we made an appointment with him to see if he could hurry a cheque along. I think I was a wee bit high-handed because I gave off about not getting the money, and we had a couple of words. He acted immediately. A cheque was there to be fetched the next day and he told the Local Enterprise Development Unit (LEDU), who'd funded us, to give us all the help we needed. Since then we've been the best of friends. Unfortunately, LEDU have not stuck to their side of the bargain because they have since let us down a couple of times.

Richard Needham, Minister for the Environment between 1985 and 1992 did, in my opinion, more for Northern Ireland than anyone else in a similar position. I've great respect for him. He's a gentleman, an Englishman and a peer, though he never accepted it (not that I know anything about peers). Both sides of the community liked him. Although he's a very busy man, whenever he comes over here he's likely to ring me and say in his smart way, 'Are you coming for coffee now, Joyce?'

The Lamplighter is a lifeline. We didn't go into it to make a profit and we've certainly had times when we have had to struggle very hard to break even, but we're still afloat. The idea was to create a few jobs at the same time as providing the Lower Ormeau Road with something that it needed. If we made a teeny weeny bit of profit that would be alright, but mainly we wanted to give people work and pay them properly.

We employ five part-time women to do all the serving, cooking and cleaning, and we have a manageress, Olive, who is overall in charge, together with another full-timer. When you consider what a full-time wage in another type of business would be, they none of them get a lot of money, but it's money they can do with and use in so many different ways. That bit extra coming into the home lifts people. A lot of the women working at the Lamplighter and upstairs at the WIDIC like to put by a small amount each week towards a Christmas hamper. They start this in July and by the time Christmas comes along there will be enough saved up for some wine, tins of biscuits, selection boxes for the kids, things to put in the stockings - all the little extras that you can't normally afford - with some money left over for the turkey. So you can have a good Christmas with no hardship or debts. And coming up to school they may be putting away so much a week for the children's uniforms. It's all sorts of things like this that can cause a lot of worry which the money helps to cover. If you're used to being middle class it's hard to understand what we're trying to do with just having a few things sorted out and a few bob extra.

We open up from ten o'clock in the morning until nine o'clock at night, long hours, because we have to work hard to pay our overheads and our wages. Not being under any scheme or grant means we have to pick up the wages every week, and it takes us all our time doing it. Workers aren't undercut either, because I think if you give them a fair wage they'll work well for you.

We also have three voluntary workers - two downstairs and one upstairs in the office - who work hard every day, too. It helps a lot. Then we have a lovely lady who comes every Monday to do the accounts, and she's been doing this a lot of years. Although she's over seventy, you'd never think it. She's as bright as a button and as honest. That's a person we're awful fond of and we would hate her to stop now.

We do big dinners at a reasonable price at the Lamplighter – a silverside roast, two veg, roast potato and boiled potato and gravy for £1.70. Now I don't know where else you'd get that. As I said, we just about break even. We have our ups and downs but we are fully determined to keep going. We try and help people out who can't afford much. Many's the free meal that goes over the counter for ones that haven't the money at the time, but they always come in and pay for it sometime later. That includes the students. I feel a pity for them in particular because I've heard landlords cram them into shabby rooms here in Belfast, the rents are high, and they don't get a good grant. The students that go to Queen's are mostly ordinary working-class sons and daughters whose parents are trying to get them through. The family can't help much, so we make sure they're filled. They love the "Special" that is on our menu each day: bacon and eggs, sausages, chips, tea, bread and butter for £2. We have even had some mothers and fathers coming down to say they're very glad there's somewhere for the students to eat where they can get such good value for money.

One of the great things about running a restaurant is the

people you meet. Certainly you'd never forget them in all your life. Mr Savage was just one of those. At eighty-odd, he came in every day for his lunch at half past twelve on the dot, and if he wasn't there we would have gone out looking for him! Every single day we were open, there would be Mr Savage. He'd been all over the world – to India, Hong Kong, you name it and he would have been there, because he was in the Army. And the yarns he used to tell!

The women in the Lamplighter were all over him for that, and he loved to flirt. He was a well-off man and an independent one, so we quickly learnt that you couldn't give him anything except if you did it in a nice way, so that he wouldn't think it was charity. I'm sure he liked coming in to us because we heard all he had to say. As a result of all his travels he never minded the heat, and in the summer, when we'd be baking and we'd be sitting outside with our sleeves rolled up, Mr Savage would be sitting inside and he'd shout out, 'You don't know what heat is. If you'd been in Hong Kong you would have melted away.'

Then Mickey started coming in; Mickey Mullin, another elderly man. He and Mr Savage used to fight. I don't mean fist fighting or anything like that; they used to argue in fun an awful lot. Mickey was jealous and he'd always be watching Mr Savage's plate. If there were one pea more he'd give off with, 'Why is he getting more than me?' Where Mickey was a big, robust pensioner – big, red cheeks and nice and fat – Mr Savage hadn't a pick on him, so we used to give him that wee bit extra to fatten him up.

They argued about the Markets area of town, the different streets that are gone now, and Mickey would say, 'That street hasn't gone – I used to live there.' Mr Savage would argue it had gone and the whole thing would turn into a row. Then it would be about their ages. Mickey would always say he was seventy-four these past three years. He had his birthday the other week so we got him a bottle of champagne, baked him a cake and we all got him a birthday card. He was delighted. But when Mickey said he was seventy-four, Mr Savage would go winking behind his back. 'Aye, seventy-four on your door,' he'd say.

Coming up to Christmas we give the pensioners in the area a bag of coal, and if we get any other extras we give them those too. We phone up different businesses and organizations and ask them if they'd donate, and very often they do. It's as much a matter of us working together as a team, and if there's anybody we think needs help, we help them.

At Christmas we bought Mr Savage socks, and cigarettes for his birthday, because he never bothered with any of his people, his family. He had cousins but they never got in touch, only, as he said 'when they're coming looking for something'. He thought he was well-off without them. One day Mr Savage took a chest infection and he went down hill badly. The year before we thought we were going to lose him, for he said he felt terrible and he failed away to nothing. But then we always made sure he had a good meal to try to make him strong. He got better eventually and filled out again. But this time he didn't improve and he had to go into hospital. When I was up there visiting him those cousins came in, and it was obvious they were only taking an interest in him because he was dying. I didn't like to see this. I'd heard Mr Savage mention that he had a daughter in England, so I got an old friend of mine, John McGarry, to write to the Salvation Army and the Irish Rifles to see if she could be traced. I believe they did trace her and she got his money, so I was content and glad about that. There was something wrong somewhere between the daughter and him, and I like to think of them making up before he died.

Many's the time since then we have looked over to the corner where Mr Savage always sat and imagined he was there. It broke our hearts to lose him. All the girls that worked in the chip shop were dying about him. God love him, he used to give one of my wee granddaughters 20p every day for her money box. 'Now you don't be touching that,' he used to say to her mother. 'You make sure it goes into her money box.' He was very fond of her and we were very fond of him. Certainly nobody will ever take his place, and he is with us in spirit.

I think Mickey missed Mr Savage too, even though they hadn't agreed with each other. But we paid him plenty of attention. When he got his dinner and his tea and toast, and after that a wee sweet, as often as not I'd say to him, 'Well, how did you enjoy your dinner Mickey?' He would say, 'It was *salubrious*', and I'd say, 'Now Mickey, some of these days I'm going to look at the dictionary to see what that means, so I hope it means *good*.'

We have our regular staff at the Lamplighter, who have been with us right from the beginning, but we also have people on community service orders that come out to do their hours with us. Jack Magee, who I've known for nine or ten years as a good friend, is in charge of that. They are usually youngsters that he brings down for us to look after, those who've done something wrong. Instead of being put in prison they opt to do something useful. I think this is a good idea because you can work alongside of them and get them to feel at home with what they're doing. It helps if you don't mind mucking in with them. There's quite a variety of jobs to be done: decorating and simple office work, cooking and cleaning, and helping to serve at the tables. Or they could be helping to grow things in the greenhouses at the back. We have found that if you respect them, they will generally respect you, and that offering them something they like doing gives them an interest.

Out of forty or fifty youngsters that have been through our hands, there was just one that we couldn't work with. He wouldn't settle down and he upset the whole outfit. He was more intelligent and he told lies, even to the Probation Officer. We reckoned he was a nasty lad who did everything to disrupt, so we shipped him somewhere else. He went to a cat and dogs' home, cleaning out the animals. I've got to say we thought he deserved it. The funny part about it was he came from a good background; there was no excuse for him to be in trouble. All the others seem to have got onto their feet, at least while they've been with us.

Although we usually get the young ones, there was just one man we had recently who was in his forties, or thereabouts. He was great; did everything; painting and cleaning, and whatever you asked him to do. The next thing we heard, from one of the girls who came into the office, was that he went in for the leather gear – bondage, I think it's called. We got to know that he liked to get himself tied to bedposts. We had a party before he'd finished his spell and he drank quite a lot of the punch we'd made. The result was he fell onto the breast of one of our working ladies and there he lay, looking down between the two as hard as ever he could. If there's a queer character in that road out there, we get them!

One day a voice rang through to the Women's Information Drop-In Centre and the person on the end said, 'Joyce, I've a wee girl with me and she won't settle anywhere'. This was an older girl apparently, past school, and she had no thought about her own future at all. 'She's from Dublin,' the voice continued, 'and I wonder if you could do anything for her.' The caller was the head of an organization that tries to fix up youngsters in great need with a place to live and something to do.

Ann came to us for about seven or eight weeks. We just made a fuss of her and let her do her own thing downstairs at the restaurant. We didn't demand too much, but we gave her a hand whenever she needed it. You have to think that people will know what to do, not tell them, and mostly they do know if you encourage them. At the end of the day Ann had decided that she liked working with young children, having seen a lot of them come to grief because they'd no stable family. She went on to do a course at Rupert Stanley College in child care, and we were all delighted about that.

Just now we have a wee boy called Billy, aged nineteen, and it's going to be a hard job with him. His mother went absent from the home and the whole family was brought up in an institution. He isn't used to being reliable and he doesn't come in every day or anywhere near it, so settling him down and finding someone that will take him on isn't going to be easy. He was in only three days in the last three weeks, but I don't pull him up for that. I just say, 'I thought you'd be in', or something like that, so as not to put too much pressure on. We'll have to see how he works out, though I'm not too hopeful.

I've always been interested in food and food values, and having so much to do with the Lamplighter gave me the push to look into these more thoroughly. This was just before the Government came out with its pamphlet called *Change of Heart*. I had also seen something on TV about a child being asthmatic and how the cheap orange juice with additives and colouring would affect it. This struck me, as one of the women who came into the Lamplighter had a child that was very asthmatic. We decided to use him as a guinea pig in what we gave him to eat. So we cut down on all the orange juices, all the sweets and anything with colouring in it, and we gave him fresh fruit and lots of fresh vegetables instead. The results were miraculous. That wee boy used to have an attack maybe once or twice a week. He didn't any more because the asthma cleared up.

We wanted to take our experiments further, and right at that moment the *Change of Heart* programme recommended all sorts of healthy things to eat. So we decided to try the healthy diet out. It made a big difference to some people, right enough, and we enjoyed all the fresh fruit and wholemeal bread, but the trouble was, most of us couldn't afford it. These things run very dear. They run to more than tinned fruit or white bread, and in my household it was impossible. We maybe eat three or four loaves a day plus a stone of potatoes and a load of veg. If we cut down on some of that and substituted the cheaper things for more expensive foods it would cost a lot more each week.

It seemed to us at the WIDIC that the Government might be recommending good things without knowing the reality of the situation for many poor families. This prompted us to do a survey to see what money a pensioner, for example, and a one-parent family had to spend on food, and how it would work out for them to change to a healthier diet. It didn't, because so many things were more costly. We wrote a booklet about our survey that was honest, and the conclusions showed that the Government hadn't really got its feet on the ground.

We also used the information to see how good people's diets were as they stood, whether they contained enough vitamins and protein, etc. We asked a professional dietitian to do this for us. She discovered that their diets were generally low on zinc and that there was another shortage: folic acid, that helps children to develop properly and makes the red cells in the blood. It made me ask if that could be why so many children from poorer families contract leukemia. If there is a connection, surely this is an area that needs looking into.

It was round about this time that my great friend Mena, who'd worked beside me and cared for me so well, got very ill. She was on inhalers for her chest. She came up to me one day and said 'Joyce, look at my hands, they're shaking so. You'd think I was an alcoholic.' 'Go up and see the doctor,' I said, 'maybe you're taking too much.' And she did. He took her off those inhalers but then her chest got worse.

Just then I'd an arrangement to go to Brussels for a poverty conference and Mena said it was important that I went. So I got everything fixed up and set off downtown Monday morning, to get a few bits and pieces. At about twelve o'clock I was back in the Centre when Mena's daughter phoned to tell me she had died. I felt so sad then. She was a lovely woman, a great worker and we always cared about the same things. I like to think that Mena died having faith in good overcoming bad. Two or three times we'd given money away that we didn't begrudge and out of the blue money had come in to replace it. 'Joyce, you know, you're right,' she used to say. 'What you give, you get back twofold.' On the day of her funeral I was on the plane to Brussels, feeling very sick. I still miss her.

∽

It might seem quite easy starting things up the way I've described, but in actual fact there's an awful lot of letter writing, meetings and paperwork that goes on behind the scenes. For instance, before you can ask for funding, more often than not, you have to have a feasibility study done. Sometimes you get the chance to do the research yourself, sometimes the requirement is that professionals are brought in. This was the case for the Lamplighter, and very annoying it was. A family of four could live for a half a year on the cost of a report done like that, and often those who write it do not listen to those who know the area well, and its needs.

As far as the training centre next door went, I wrote to the estate agents that were handling the building and asked them to hold onto it until we could raise some money. They wrote back saying 'a bird in the hand is worth two in the bush' – those are the very words they used! – and sold it. But I was determined. I found out who bought it and invited them down for a cup of tea. Before that cup of tea had vanished we'd bought it off them. This is as true as God made us eyes to see! But we still had no money. We raised it, as quickly as we could, through different Trusts and people who believed in what we were doing. Cadbury's were more than generous. Somehow or other we got hold of what we needed and we called it Mornington Enterprises. Why? Because there used to be a factory nearby called Mornington where young ones worked. It offered a lot of jobs before it got burnt down in the Troubles.

It was when we were looking for staff to run Mornington Enterprises that I first met Janice, my full-time assistant. She came to me after Mena's death, partly because the work had been mounting up, and partly to give me that extra bit of technical help that I needed. Janice is a very special person, so innocent for her age, with a lovely face and beautiful, regular teeth. I knew immediately that she was a very caring person and that, if Mornington couldn't use her, I would want her working with me. I talked to her two or three times and liked her whole attitude. She had a good degree behind her from Queen's and all the experience in research that we could ever need. As it happened, the sort of Government funding scheme that Mornington was under didn't allow for a full-time assistant's salary, so Janice came to me.

A year went past with us working together and by that time we started to blend with me putting the ideas forward and Janice putting them down on paper, each of us needing the other. Over the years, five now, I've seen her develop and I think she's learnt a lot, coming from a quiet family that didn't want her to see too much of the rougher side of life. Now we're like Siamese twins, with a good, warm friendship. I think the only reason I'll lose Janice is because someone will want to marry her. It's my personal hope that he'll be damned near perfect, which is what she deserves.

Mornington Enterprises runs quite separately from the WIDIC and the Lamplighter, although it is right next door. It offers training to young people in the eighteen-plus age range and is now fully funded by the Government under the ACE programme. There is a good choice of training in computers, gardening, painting and decorating, woodwork and catering. It's all very practical. The caterers help to run a thriving coffee shop on the ground floor which provides snacks and sandwiches to the public as well as trainees and staff.

Unfortunately, the young ones are only in there for a year, and in my opinion that is not long enough to settle them down and stop them going back onto the streets. They're only just beginning to learn a skill when they're out. I'd like to see more time spent on training youngsters so that by the time they leave they really know what it is they've been trained for. They should be caught earlier too. By the time you get to eighteen a lot of bad habits can have set in. We have recently done a feasibility study at WIDIC which looks at the needs of fifteen to nineteen-year-olds very carefully, and we have high hopes that we can provide a scheme that really fits them.

Having said all this, I recently went over to Mornington

when a whole batch of young ones received their certificates. I must say, I felt as proud as punch sitting there watching the ceremony. Over twenty went through these last few months and the schemes are being expanded the whole time. Already there are thirteen Action for Community Employment (ACE) workers and one full-salaried, employed person. So apart from the training schemes, it's provided a lot of local employment.

As with all my projects, I couldn't have done a thing without the help of the good people that have worked alongside of me. When it came to advertising for a manager who could build up a training centre, a certain young man came along. He looked the right type to me, the best man for the job, but when we brought him back for a chat, to let him know he'd done well in the interview and that we wanted him, he said to me, 'Why are you giving this job to me, a Protestant?' I said, 'I'm not interested in your religion; whether you're a Protestant or a Hindu or a Catholic. All I'm interested in is can you train young people and encourage them, give them a skill so that they'll have a future?' He said 'Yes' so I forgot about being angry with him for making that weird comment and forgave him. Our choice was right, of that I'm sure. If Ken hadn't been just the right man, there's no way Mornington would be going so smoothly.

Apart from him, a lot of its success has been due to John Coote of the Riverside Action Team. John has now moved on to other things but we owe a lot to him. Every year he'll come for a drink at Christmas. We get a bottle of Olde Bushmills whiskey, Black Bush, especially for him. We didn't receive any support or interest from the local business community, but John had the vision and the confidence to know that the local people would help us out at every stage, and he supported us.

I have been delighted to see this project doing so well, not only for the sake of the young ones, but also for the sake of Janice and myself. By the time it took off we had plenty more coming onto our plates from other directions, and not all of it work either.

∽

SEVEN

America and Other Journeys

Loads of people enjoy travelling and they get a lot out of it. Perhaps they see what they want to see and not what they don't. I'm not one of those. For a start, when I'm abroad I keep thinking, 'I wonder what is going on at home.' And 'Should I be there?' On top of that, I have a habit of getting involved with things that are definitely not on the tourist map. Usually, I'm side-tracked by people, their circumstances and what they are trying to do. For these reasons the biggest journey I ever did in my life so far, to America, turned out very different from the way it was supposed to be.

In 1990 I went to America to raise funds for our projects in Belfast. Half a million I was after, and since the Americans have always kept up strong connections with Ireland and there had also been a lot of interest in our work coming from over there, I made the decision to go.

As always, there was an awful lot of paperwork to do to get it all arranged. It was businessmen I wanted to see, so we approached a number of organizations and individuals in Northern Ireland who we thought could get us some sympathetic contacts in the States, including the Society of Friends, the Northern Ireland Bureau and the Belfast Action Team. They came up with people in New York, Boston, Philadelphia and Washington who wanted to meet me. Because there was no way I was going to do all this on my own,

I asked Ann McAllister from Business in the Community to come with me.

We had a brochure prepared that set out what we were trying to do to improve the area of the Lower Ormeau Road through Mornington Enterprises and the WIDIC, and what the American people could do to help us. That went out in advance, to prepare the way for the talks I was to give to all those smart individuals and organizations. When I saw the itinerary I nearly collapsed for trying to imagine how I was going to keep up with only two days in each place. But as it turned out it was not that side of the trip that was to cause me such trouble.

I might as well have left the planet altogether by the time I got to New York - that is what it felt like anyway, with all those buildings towering above me. I had a meeting with some businessmen there and I said my say, but what they thought of me I couldn't tell. Then I had some time in which to wander about a bit with Ann. The impression I got was that it was all rush. Nobody seemed to have time for anyone else; you never saw anybody greet another person and it didn't seem to me the sort of place where you could stand talking to a friend on the pavement. And all this in amongst such big skyscrapers. I didn't like it and I didn't think I could possibly live there. Boston was almost as bad, with people hurrying everywhere, only the buildings were more normal.

Then we got to Washington. After another one of my talks a man came up and invited me to a drop-in centre which wasn't on the schedule, but I thought I should go. When I got there it nearly broke my heart, so many people with HIV positive - young girls expecting babies and young men. The place was full of them: it seems like a lot of people have no time for relatives with AIDS-related conditions. I met one young girl there who sticks in my mind, a wee coloured girl I got talking to. She told me that her husband was in gaol, where he would be for the next year or so, because he had broken probation. It must have been for a drug offence or something like that. Here she was HIV positive, and ten to one the baby would be HIV positive too. I took to her an awful lot; you couldn't help but let your heart go out to someone in that wee girl's position. There were only so many dollars in my purse but I got out the lot and gave them to her. I couldn't think how else to help her.

We stayed for lunch in the centre and they were all delighted that we were eating together. There was a young lad I got talking to after we'd eaten. He was HIV positive too and had taken drugs. When we were going, he put out his hand to shake mine but instead I put my arms around him and gave him a hug because I wanted him to know I wasn't afraid to touch him. He cried and I cried. I was sure that those people must have felt like aliens, being stuck away so ill and so isolated. It didn't seem the best way to cure them to me, treating them like lepers, and I decided to do whatever I could for them when I got home.

I met Mother Hayle there. She was a marvellous person who looked after the babies that were born with AIDS. She died last year, but what a Godsend she was. I couldn't imagine anybody else taking on the job that she did with such a lot of good spirit and warmth.

That night I was due to meet some more businessmen to ask for funding, but I couldn't go ahead with it. It was so sad to see so much poverty in America. I'd seen so many homeless and miserable by then; people eating out of bins, people lying over the grids in the road to warm themselves at night. I felt sickened. So I stood up and said to the businessmen, 'Charity begins at home'. I told them I couldn't ask for help because

America had too many problems, and that I felt ashamed coming there with the idea of getting money off them. You could have cut the air with a knife when I was talking, but it had to be said, even though most of them didn't like to hear it. I left the country with plenty of addresses from interested parties, but I never ever could bring myself to apply for funding to a single one of them, despite our own needs.

At the same time as upsetting the businessmen I fell out with a good friend of mine who was working with some Irish people, mostly the wives of men on the run in Northern Ireland who'd escaped to America. These women had followed their husbands and stayed on too long, their visas had run out and they'd lost their passports. They couldn't apply for work permits and this meant they were open to being abused. On the quiet, they were getting work organized by my friend but they weren't getting paid properly for doing it. I told my friend she was taking advantage of their situation and she replied, 'Well, they wouldn't get money otherwise.' 'But that's not the point. It's the principle of the thing,' I said.

I met some of them and they were anxious. Even if their mother had died they wouldn't have been able to get home because they had no passport, so they were telling me. Some days later I was invited to tea with the Vice Consul for Ireland and I remember giving off to him with, 'It's not fair. If your mother or father died and you couldn't get back to them how would you feel?' You know, if you talk right and you don't let on that you are what you're not, you can get a long way. I'm glad to say some months later passports were issued to them, so that was at least something we accomplished.

I would hate to see Northern Ireland go the way of America: no time even to say hello and everyone going hither and thither so fast. It felt wrong to me and I guess it's affecting families over there even more than it is with us. I strongly believe in the family unit, where daughters can go to their mammies for help and to their grannies too, for that matter; where the whole family is intact. You might have your ups and downs but it's between one another, and still with all, it's family.

It was a ten-day trip – ten days too much. I was disgusted. I couldn't get home quick enough, for I'd had my eyes opened. New York was the worst. I never saw poverty like that before or since. It was quite a shock after imagining for so long that America was the land of plenty. In a way I was sorry Janice hadn't been with me on that trip because we would have been able to share some of the experiences and talk about them afterwards. Perhaps more would have come out of it if we had, but I doubt it.

As soon as I got home I arranged to meet some of the women who came into the WIDIC. We got together and started a sewing workshop upstairs in one of the attic rooms. We set to and made a big tortoise from different coloured felts that a child could sit on, and we balloted it and sent all the money to America, to the AIDS drop-in centre. Our thoughts went with it, and let's hope it did some good. I wouldn't forget the kindness and the hospitality we got in the States from all the people who had us to stay. Nor would I forget the one big lesson we learnt: There's people worse off than us, and so long as we stick together, we'll always get by.

∞

There are few people can say they've been presented with awards by two of the most powerful women in England and Ireland. It would be dishonest if I were to say I wasn't proud of being one of them. The first great occasion, leading up to these, was meeting Mary Robinson, the President of the Irish

Republic. She is a unique lady, being more in touch with the ordinary people than any other person I know in such a high position. The first time I went up to meet Mary was at her house in Dublin, along with some others from the Women's Information Group. We had a great afternoon sitting in the garden of the President's House, and she brought me all around to see the grounds and showed me a tree Queen Victoria planted when she visited Ireland. At one point we were in the drawing room and I was there in the chair that President Kennedy sat on during one of his visits. I had to say to Mary, didn't it just fit me grand! What is so lovely about her is that you can tease her and she'll laugh, and she'll make everyone feel important. That is a great gift, specially with people in power. It's just a pity there aren't more have it.

The second time I met Mary was for the presentation of the Pensioner of the Year Award, North and South, organized by Irish Life Insurance in 1991. Some time before this occasion I had had a letter asking me to fill in details of what work I was doing in Belfast. Janice had done the best she could with it. We hadn't given it much thought, either at the time or afterwards, and the next thing we heard was that I was in the finals. These were being held in Dublin.

I went down there with a friend of mine, Vera, and we were put up in a great, plush hotel, the Gresham, which was gorgeous. That first night we were longing for a wee drink but we didn't know how to go about getting one so we did without. In the morning we asked one of the others what we should have done and she said, 'Why didn't you lift the phone and ask for one to be brought up? Ring down,' she said, 'everything's paid for.'

The next day we had to go round to be interviewed by a panel from the radio and the TV, and there were journalists waiting to ask us about ourselves for the papers. When I looked around I thought all the others were speaking so well and sounding so polite and sure of themselves. I didn't see that I was much like them and I said to Vera, 'I'm just going to go on and be myself.' We were all runners-up but nobody knew yet who the winner would be.

When it came to it, we were all sitting at the front of the stage and Mary Robinson was going to make the presentation. Someone read through the whole list of us: what we'd done and where, what our interests were, and so on. Then there was a pause and out it came: 'Joyce McCartan, Pensioner of the Year'. It was such a lovely surprise because I hadn't thought for a moment that I'd be chosen. Then immediately I had to go up to get the prize of two beautiful, big, glass vases of Waterford crystal. I had a long, pink skirt on and I had to go up the steps real quick, and didn't I lose my shoe and trip! They must all have thought that I was half-tipsy, but I'd no drink in me at the time. All I could do was laugh.

I was so overwhelmed by the whole thing that when I had to make my speech it just didn't come out. It was then that Mary Robinson immediately gave me a hand. She said 'You know, when Joyce came down to see me a lot of weeks ago she was advising me what way to treat women. She didn't lose her speech then.' So I began to speak, but what I said, I can't recall.

Afterwards, when we got back to the hotel, me and Vera thought we deserved a drink so we lifted the phone. Acting like two well-to-do people, we ordered a couple of vodkas to be brought up the stairs. We got what we wanted without any trouble at all and it was a great way to end the day.

During the rest of the stay we had plenty of opportunities to meet people and made some lasting friendships. We got to know one doctor well, Dr Jim Deeney, and to this day I've a great respect for him. He had a friend, Dr Noel Brown, who he talked about an awful lot. They used to work together. He, himself, was advisor on health to the Pope and the European Parliament, and Dr Noel Brown was a great man for women's ailments. He related how Dr Brown's mother had died of TB, and his sisters too, and how he'd come over to Ireland years ago to help bring poor women into the wards so that they could have their babies more safely. Dr Noel Brown had seen an awful lot of hardship with women and all he'd wanted to do was to better them.

Then the Church suddenly turned against him and called him a communist. The very Church did that! This was a real genuine person and his heart was all for improving the health of women. I thought to myself at the time, 'I've fought for the poor all my life, including myself, and I wouldn't say I'm a communist any more than Dr Noel Brown.' It made me wonder how those who are supposed to be caring could be so ignorant. I took my hat off to both these good doctors for just carrying on without bitterness.

Each year now I get an invitation to attend the Pensioner of the Year Awards and I look forward to meeting the same few people again and again. I go down to Dublin praying that all of them will be there, but there's always one or two missing. Dr Jim Deeney is up in years, but, thank God, he's still going strong.

The next grand occasion was when I got the MBE, which was presented to me in London at Buckingham Palace. I nearly blew, getting a letter all of a sudden in November 1992 asking me if I'd accept it. I was delighted, although I couldn't think who had put me up for it or why, as I didn't see I had done anything that terrific.

At the time I had just finished doing something for radio.

Susan Marling and Merrilyn Harris had been over making a programme called *The Kitchen Cabinet*. When they finished that they came back to ask me to do *Joyce's Scrapbook*, about daily events in and around the Ormeau Road. That was around October. Just when the recording was done we heard about the MBE and Susan and Merrilyn decided to treat me to a hat. Put it this way, it's seldom I wear a hat and absolutely never that I thought I would need one to meet the Queen. I couldn't go by myself to choose one, because I hadn't ever owned a hat since I was a wee girl, so I asked my good friend Sally McErlean to come with me.

Sally is one of my oldest and best friends in Belfast. She didn't have a lot of schooling but this has never stopped her doing a great job helping adolescent boys and girls in difficulty, and advising the families. Apart from being a terrific worker, she's one of the best laughs out. She could make a donkey laugh, sure she could! I knew Sally would welcome a trip out to one of the swankiest shops in town, so we opted for the hat shop that Princess Di had opened just a few weeks before. We nearly brought the house down with trying all the different hats on, both of us, before settling on which one to have. Finally, I got this grey one and it looked awful well on me, though I'm saying it myself. I still have it and it's very precious to me. I keep it on top of the wardrobe, though it comes out on special occasions.

Janice and I were soon over to London for the presentation ceremony, with all the smart gear we would need packed up in a couple of suitcases. We went a few days early because we wanted to do some other work before the event. We stayed right opposite the Zoo in a gorgeous, big house belonging to Eddie Lawlor. He's a man who has helped to fund so many of our projects so generously. We had a lovely time roaming around London, eating terrific food and shopping. Susan Marling came for us and took us out to dinner, and we went to the House of Lords where we met Lord Blease of Cromac and Dr T. B. F. Thompson from Garvagh, who hosted a special cross-community peace conference for representatives from Northern Ireland.

Going into the Palace was very exciting indeed. It's beautiful. And you want to see the paintings! I could have stayed all day and gone round all the walls looking at and appreciating them. I'm glad it's open to the public because it gives an opportunity for a lot of people to see so many wonderful things. If they can be enjoyed, why should they be hoarded and hidden away?

When I got as far as meeting the Queen I had to make a wee bow and shake her hand. To be quite honest, I didn't know what to do, but to my surprise she seemed to know all about me and my work. We talked for a couple of minutes. You couldn't help but admire the way she managed to say something to each one of us and get it right. After that she pinned the MBE onto my jacket. You're then supposed to back out, but I forgot, and rushed off frontwards. 'Well, anyone can make a mistake,' I thought to myself, and I'm sure she must have understood. All the same, I couldn't help wondering what my friends were thinking as they sat in the audience watching.

I thought the Queen was a lovely woman, with gorgeous skin that reminded me of my mother-in-law's. She did look a bit worried and I pitied her, for she was going through a very tough time with her family just then. What makes me angry, if I think about it, is that mothers are made to feel completely responsible for their children. Whether it's the Queen or some ordinary woman, it makes no difference. I hope things sort out for her and that she doesn't feel it's all her fault, because it won't be.

My medal is a silver cross, done up with a striped ribbon and laid in a satin-lined box. I treasure it greatly. Although I've been a battler all my life, I never thought I'd get to meet the Queen. It's a great achievement for me and a great honour - one I'll never forget.

The other journeys I've made in the last few years have been shorter than the American trip. So far I've never failed to find at least bits of them interesting, and often I've been personally affected and learnt a great deal. Going to Dublin - back and forth several times with Janice to fix up a Women's Information Group there - has always been worthwhile, with the women being so enthusiastic and go-ahead. We get on so well together, I can't imagine why our small island should be at all divided.

Recently I visited Docklands, in London. I was struck by the many mistakes that were made there that could be repeated when they start developing the gasworks in Belfast. I met loads of women who felt that their community and the jobs for their men had been destroyed by the yuppie building plans; offices and houses for the rich that weren't even being used. We all know what a huge amount of money went into the Canary Wharf development, but who knows or cares about the amount of misery it has caused the residents? Let's hope the Laganside Corporation, who are working on the river improvement here in Belfast, make themselves aware of how wrong things can go. They could do worse than use the Docklands model as a warning.

Some of the trips I've done have just been great fun. For example, the time we went down to Ballyshannon to take a look at the Shannon Enterprises to see if we could learn anything for our work. That's an awful big enterprise, incidentally, with millions of pounds of Government money going into renovating old buildings and making them look as good as they used to. It was very interesting looking around. Then in the evening we were taken to Bunratty Castle for a huge banquet. The food was grand, and we had a lot of fun playing 'kings and queens' in the mediaeval setting. It was a really lovely evening.

Although I enjoy smart occasions and travelling, especially doing the exchanges with other women, I never feel quite right being away from the Ormeau Road. I always return home thinking, 'That's where I'm needed and where I prefer to be.'

❧

EIGHT

The Way Ahead

You would think now that I'm getting towards the end of my life story, and beginning to look forward rather than back, there'd be no more horrible events to relate. But one there is. It cannot be left out because from it has grown a lot that could be wonderful.

There is a practice or punishment, whatever you choose to call it, in Northern Ireland that is done by thugs and terrorists to each other and also to innocent people. It is called kneecapping. I know someone who got kneecapped. He was the best fellow out, and it had a terrible effect on him. It shatters the whole knee, and in his case he has a hole as big as your fist in his leg. Some of them lose their legs, but God's been good and this one didn't. Now why it happened I don't know. But one thing is sure – it turned him into an alcoholic. It's a son of mine I'm talking about.

He'd been babysitting with his wee Protestant friend, just up the road from us, when they got broken into. They were held by a couple of thugs for hours and all the time they didn't know if they'd come out alive. Then they each got kneecapped. By the time I heard about it and got up there all I could see was big clots of blood like liver going along the pavement, and them getting into the ambulance. You lose an awful lot of blood with having your knees blown out at close range, and you could die of it. I felt sick.

I went everywhere, in and out of all the bars in the area asking, 'What did my son do to get kneecapped?' I was so angry that night that if I'd have got hold of them they would have died in my grip and I'm not a violent person. We put it in the papers. We couldn't give the name of the two lads involved for fear of reprisals, but we did all we could to give it publicity. Nobody claimed responsibility but I think the reason it happened was connected with the kind of work I do, trying to help families on both sides of the community.

Eventually something of a response did come back, in a roundabout way, from those who did it – a message which said, 'If you can think of anything better for us, we'll stop the kneecapping.' So I've come up with something better: a feasibility study for a fifteen to nineteen-year-olds' skills development scheme, to be sited in the old gasworks development area.

When I first came to live in Belfast the gasworks site was a busy, dirty, noisy place employing about 3,000 people. Now there's nobody, and all twenty-five acres of it lie empty and derelict. It's made a huge difference to the Ormeau Road. We've got to put something in its place that will cater for the communities.

The people living around the gasworks put up with a lot when it was functioning. Often the bad health of their children was blamed on the fumes that came off the site. All the same, the fact that it was there gave them a lot of benefits as well. There were the trains that went chugging along the back of the houses, heaped up with hills of black coal. That was the coal being brought to make the gas. You were lucky if you had your house on the railway side of the road. If you were quick you came out and put a brush over the wall and knocked some of the lumps off the top. Whatever fell off you put by, so it helped people to survive in hard times.

Because so many people lived and worked close at hand, the Markets area around the gasworks was a thriving place of stalls and shops. There was Inglis's Bakery, I remember, where you used to get fresh bread for next to nothing, and when they'd finished selling at the end of the day they'd often chuck the remaining loaves out for free. We had a butter and egg shop, and lovely fresh vegetables that had just come in from the country, a saddler and a drapers. It was a great place to shop. Now they're all gone and they're badly missed.

We at the WIDIC have a vision for the site itself. Training schemes on their own are not enough – they need to be set in a new environment, one that can give employment and a whole new lift to the people. All that derelict land is in an ideal spot and could be developed for the benefit of the five communities that live around it, having suffered the stink and dirt for so long. The gasworks is in a neutral position, right in the middle of two Protestant communities and three that are Catholic. So it's mixed and almost equal. It's the one place where I can say we could build on that neutral/mixed factor, and both sides could benefit. It's a huge area and is quite near the centre of town. All we are looking for is thirteen acres, and that is only half the total.

You may be wondering how a whole lot of women set about making a plan on such a grand scale. We heard of a suggestion to put up more offices, but considering Belfast is full of empty offices that aren't getting let right now, we didn't agree with that. You might not believe it, but as a result we women sat round a table and asked ourselves, 'What do we need now in this area? What would we like to see? What would bring money and work in?' We realized, for example, we have no banks around here, and only a very small post office. So we need a bigger post office and a bank, where you still get served efficiently like you used to. There is hardly any space set aside for children to play in for miles around, so we need a playground. I think a city farm is very important for youngsters, because when they work along with animals it makes them more caring, so, a city farm. And a few more things: a car park and a shopping centre, to create some competition for the shopping centre we have up the other end of Ormeau Road.

So, how does the long-term skills development scheme for fifteen to nineteen-year-olds fit into the gasworks project? Mainly, it would provide a realistic setting in which young people could develop a large range of skills according to their choice. It would take them out of school, where so many of them have failed, into the outside world, where what they produced could be marketed and what they contributed in labour could be waged.

The next thing we worked on was a proposal document, outlining the sort of scheme we thought right for the young people in question. Here, briefly, is what we wrote:

THE LOCATION

The Lower Ormeau is approximately half a mile square, not inclusive of the twenty-five acre gasworks site, with over 8,000 residents. The area is characterized by a high degree of economic and social deprivation due to low incomes, lack of space, lack of amenities, and ill-health.

The fundamental issue in the Lower Ormeau involves regeneration of the area and the prevention of the further spread of decay, along with the restoration of an economic base capable of sustaining the future generation, which consists mostly of very young families. What is essential for the area is a complete programme of action for change which is both visionary and pragmatic.

Responsible for the regeneration of Lower Ormeau is the Riverside Action Team, a Government initiative administered by the Department of the Environment in Northern Ireland. Riverside are currently working along with the Laganside Corporation (responsible for redevelopment of the gasworks site) to assist the community financially in its attempt to acquire a part of the gasworks site for redevelopment purposes.

The twenty-five acre gasworks site has just recently undergone a process of detoxification to prepare the ground for redevelopment purposes. The preparation of this site has cost the Department of Economic Development the approximated sum of £3m (the final figure has not yet been reached). There have been a number of different suggestions for usage of the site which Laganside have received as a result of consultation with the five surrounding communities.

The Klondyke building is currently housing a Job Training Programme (JTP) scheme, financed by the Training and Employment Agency, and initially promoted by the Construction Industry Training Board (CITB). This will provide training in construction and building for local adults for when the redevelopment process begins in the gasworks. What the scheme fails to cater for is sixteen-year-olds, of which there are a high number in the local area. It is important to consider this age group, who more readily learn skills than the older generation.

THE SITUATION

Many sixteen-year-olds leave school with the feeling that they are unworthy. They have drifted through the education system with no real knowledge of why, have received no careers guidance, and can see no future on the job market. The education received is not sufficient for all young people; it does not provide practical experience for those who do not understand paperwork. There is a void between primary and secondary school levels for some children – not all are academically minded, but are just punching their time in. These are the children who are neglected by the educational system. This is just the beginning of a vicious circle for the majority of young people. They go on to look for a job either with or without qualifications. The constant cry from employers is that you cannot get a job without experience. Yet you cannot get experience without a job. Only the highly qualified get jobs, and even those are few and far between. Even some children with mediocre qualifications lose hope, with a lack of incentive to continue on with their education, and a fear of looking for work which they won't like.

Given the fact that there are a limited number of places on government training schemes, the Government cannot claim to make adequate provision for our sixteen to eighteen-year-olds. According to the booklet *Get Into Training and Employment*, produced by the Training and Employment Agency, YTP offers young people an integrated two-year programme of full-time training with employment designed to meet individual needs. All sixteen and seventeen-year-olds can enter the programme regardless of qualifications. What the booklet omits to point out is that there is a limited number of spaces on YTP programmes. There is also a lack of incentive for sixteen-year-olds who have received no benefit from continuing their education. YTP also offers a seemingly comprehensive set of skills-related programmes. Yet, if we talk to numerous young people of sixteen, few can pinpoint anything they see as worthwhile.

It is the dropouts that suffer the most. If they do not get onto YTP, the family suffers by having to support another adult. This leads to hardship in the home, rows, and the young person eventually falls away from the family. More importantly, it is the mothers of these young people who have to suffer the most – they have to provide food, clothing, and money for other expenses. The whole family suffers as a result of this, as one dependent sixteen-year-old pulls the whole family further into deprivation.

With the added strain on the young person – family rows, no money, and the influence of their friends – they begin to experiment with the social evils:

- drugs
- alcohol
- petty crime
- vandalism

and more seriously, they become prone to the influence of the paramilitaries. Once involved, they quickly go down the road of ruination.

THE ALTERNATIVE

It is our responsibility, as the older generation, to mind young people into developing their skills, then into secure work and adult life. Sarah Boseley reports on an alternative system adopted by the French, which gets to the base of the problem:

> When the French talk about crime prevention, they mean something very different from Neighbourhood Watch schemes. Most of their efforts are focused on young people who have never committed a crime. They are working on what are the root causes of crime – unemployment, failure at school, bad housing, and family difficulties. The French approach says that young people living on low-income estates, from families with no money for holidays, must be given something to do. In Toulouse, the councils fund workshops for the repair of bicycles, motorbikes, scooters and cars on housing estates both for the use of local youngsters and also to provide some with jobs.

We should be encouraging young people to find out what they can do. Every person has a skill. Once they have realized they can do something and reach competence at that, then it is time to consider how they can work education in along with it and build on what is a solid base of learned knowledge.

If we look at all the various skills young people could have, skills which are not even considered by the educational process, a whole new arena opens up. What we need to do is to find out what young people are interested in, what they do in their spare time, and what they would like to do. We need to find something in them which will spark off a talent. At present, the educational system only serves to suppress life skills, by keeping children away from practical skills and what they enjoy most. In order to give people self-respect, they need to be doing the things they enjoy successfully, and making something useful and worthwhile happen. People can regain their self-esteem just by having a pay packet at the end of the week, but it would be much more satisfying to work at something enjoyable for that remuneration.

We need to pay more attention to our young, and show them that someone cares. We need to be able to produce evidence that getting to the root problems will reduce crime, vandalism, substance abuse and paramilitary involvement.

A well-supported community can mean the difference between deprivation and success.

A PRACTICAL SOLUTION

In contrast to Government training schemes, which last only one to two years with little remuneration, we aim to provide a three-year, on-the-job, skills-related scheme, which will be self-sustaining, eventually, and which will produce some paid employment. We will begin to encourage students, during their final year at secondary school, to do day-release with our project. At this stage, many face a life of unemployment. The scheme will then employ sixteen to nineteen-year-olds who have no interest in furthering their education, but who do have a lot of ability for practical work. Each year they will receive an annual rise, in line with inflation, in order to show appreciation for their work and to help give them some self-respect. The produce from the scheme must be shown to be useful, so we will investigate the potential market in due course.

The young people will be given full instruction in sculpting, reupholstery, painting, interior design, and many other artistic talents, which will open up a whole new market for tourism in the Lower Ormeau area. The most important part of the scheme is that it will give sixteen to nineteen-year-olds an interest in their work, in themselves, and in life in general; it will keep them off the streets and out of trouble; they will become more employable, and more aware of the working situation.

Once they are in their final year they will receive careers guidance to help them make a choice between continuing with further education, joining the world of work, or setting up on their own. Whatever happens, we will give them the full support they need, and try to prevent them from losing hope.

This has to be a very special project, a paragon, where care and support is implemented at all stages of the scheme. We, as parents in the community, know that it will work, and that if it is successful, a whole series of schemes could follow suit. We know that this can be successful because it will be set up by the people for their own sons and daughters, and that this will be a perfect example for people in other areas.

To provide more details on the needs of this age group we had a feasibility study, that covered the whole of Belfast, done by a professional researcher. There is nothing in that to tell us we are on the wrong road. On the contrary, our proposal and the recommendations of the study agree very well. Like us, it emphasizes the need for the very best instructors, those that are prepared to put their hearts into the work and are really interested in young adults that need a lot of attention. This really is the key to the scheme. Without the exceptional teachers it would fail, as so many have before it.

Quite a lot of the research for other aspects of the gasworks development is being done by us, and we're getting about as much as we can to see how other people are running similar projects.

The trotting track is one of the most important things we've planned – central to the whole scheme – and we know enough now to say it is a very popular idea with the local people. We are hoping to put one in which could double up as a football pitch and an outside sports arena. Janice and I have been up and down to Dublin with the gasworks plans. We've seen Liam Wallace, who owns a trotting track, and he tells us if we could get the land and make the track we could twin with the Republic of Ireland and compete with horses from France and England. It is a thriving sport and, along with the trotting competitions and displays, we could hold a Donkey Derby and an annual fair like they used to have years ago, where horses were sold. People would come from all over Ireland for that. We've met some businessmen in Dublin who run a trotting track together with a golf putting set-up and they make a lot of money. There's no reason why the two wouldn't work for us in Belfast, where there's plenty of space for both. This is our *vision*, and we think it a good one, for it would bring such closeness to the communities.

There are a lot of things people miss these days that didn't have to disappear. Some of the old crafts which Ireland has always been famous for could be encouraged and practised in workshops on the premises – not just for show, but to be sold to visitors and tourists. Lacemaking, hand knitting, pottery, woodcarving, leather works, silversmithing and engraving, weaving and tapestry – I would hate to see the skills that go into these die out. Something else we have thought about. To see horses being shod you have to go away into the countryside. We could have a blacksmith in our back yard in the Ormeau Road, for youngsters need to know where things come from and what goes into them without having to travel too far. Using the gasworks site like this would give them a good chance to learn a lot and even try out some of the crafts themselves and see if they were interested.

The Klondyke is a big, big, massive building on the site which is also partly used as a museum. We want to get hold of enough of it to put on theatre shows and concerts. Recently, the Opera House in central Belfast was so badly damaged by a bomb that it couldn't open. *West Side Story* was coming up for showing, produced by young ones from all over Northern Ireland and England, and right at the last moment it had to be transferred. The Klondyke building was chosen and could have been made for it. It was a great success.

Another event was planned for the Klondyke after that, but it didn't happen. One day a big advertisement went up on so many billboards about a rave party that was going to be held there. It was going to attract young people from everywhere. Our experience of rave told us that drugs are sometimes introduced, and we were quite angry about it. So we all rang up the councillors in the City Hall to say we didn't want a party like that and it should be stopped. One of the councillors told us they were having a meeting that night and he would put our objections forward. Well, it was cancelled then and there and we were all delighted. We don't want things like that, bringing harm to people. The building is so fine and large it deserves to be used for everyone's benefit.

If we got part of the Klondyke I would like to see the youngsters on the fifteen-plus development programme helping to convert it, so that they would take pride in it and wouldn't do anything to hurt it. They would look after it and have a feeling for it. The only way I can see things getting built and not being touched in Catholic or Protestant areas is with the communities being involved. Only then will they stay up.

So the plan we made for the gasworks incorporates a mixture of business, heritage, tourism and pleasure, as well as being a skills development centre. We see the development as a village, with small craft shops, banks, post offices, offices for those working to help run the project, a museum, theatre, banquet hall, pubs, markets, workshops, a city farm, stables, a shopping centre, training college and a play area for the kids. There is already a lot of government-funded work going on to improve the riverside. Along with this, the tourist industry would receive a great boost with a boat service on the River Lagan taking people on trips. But even without the tourists, we all agree that it's about time the ordinary people got something in return for the discomfort they have experienced for so long, living where they do.

It is three years since our plan was completed and sent up to central government, but we've had no response yet. We are still waiting to hear what is to happen and praying that we might get a chance to make our vision a reality, providing we can get enough investment from outside sources, of course. We think we *can*. We won't give up anyway, we'll keep on fighting.

If our scheme gets accepted, and we can set it up in the gasworks, I'm hoping to work with the young ones. They are the ones, beginning at around fifteen, who don't want to go onto further education and the most likely to be drawn into trouble. The fact is, we ourselves have not taken enough interest in our young and, God help them, they're getting condemned all over. We've thrown them aside; we've closed our eyes to youngsters that weren't scholars and we haven't put enough money and enthusiasm into the right places to help them.

Our other big project, we are determined will work, is called The Five Acorns. Out of little acorns grow mighty oak trees. Since there are five plans we want to set up in one building, and we know they will grow, we thought that was a good name.

It's a bar right next door to us that we want to convert. It is an 'L' shape and there's an awful lot of room in it. If you leave a place empty it always deteriorates and this one looks terrible. At the present moment it's an eyesore and it spoils the row it's in, where there are three shops which look very well together: a privately owned cigarette shop, then Mornington Enterprises, and next to that the Lamplighter Fish and Chip Café. We could have bought and made something of it a long time ago, only the owner has wanted three times the money the bar is worth. He's been greedy, and the Government isn't that soft that it would buy something so overpriced. But in the end the price will come down, it will have to. Then we hope to buy the bar and turn it into all the things we want it to be.

The Belfast Action Team and the Laganside Corporation are going to try and make the area all round the river yuppie. They're cleaning it up and making it nice so that boats can go on it, and turning the walkways into pleasant places where you can take a stroll. I don't mind all that, so long as the community gets the use of it and it's not too expensive to take the family out on a boat at the weekend. But if it's going to be yuppie country in the river area, then we in the community are going yuppie too. I want people to come from outside and spend their money so that it can stay to build up the Lower Ormeau Road.

If you want to attract people, you have to offer them something good and you have to give them a choice. Our Five Acorns plan has been designed with that in mind, as well as providing the local people with some much-needed amenities.

The costs have risen sharply because of the bad repair of the building. It isn't even structurally sound, according to a survey commissioned by the WIDIC, which makes the asking price even more ridiculous. When we first started planning the Five Acorns we were thinking in hundreds of pounds, then we went into thousands, and by the look of it now it's going to go on to millions. It's scaring the pants off me! The likes of us that are not used to big money find it frightening, getting involved with such large sums. Thank God there are a couple of good auditors that do the books, so that everything is kept above board. If that were not the case I doubt if we would get other people's backing. But, keeping up our hopes, we have been working hard to get the funding and we still believe that all five projects will one day be firmly rooted.

Under the heading *Proposals for 1994*, in the annual report which was circulated from the WIDIC recently, the five projects are described as:

Community Hostel

In the whole of Northern Ireland there exist only six youth hostels, one of which is situated in the Ravenhill area of Belfast. Each year, we have hundreds of visitors who need places to stay, to carry out their studies or just generally to get to know our country. We have several women's groups who visit each year, but who are restricted in their visits because of the high costs of accommodation. Our premises are situated just walking distance away from both the Botanic and Central train stations, is on the main bus route to the south east of Ireland, and is part of an area which is in the process of redevelopment as a major tourist area and an extension to the city centre. The aim of the hostel will be to provide a service to everyone, whilst creating jobs for local people.

Cross-Community Conference Centre

Within the premises at 113 Ormeau Road there is a very large lounge which was previously used to hold functions, such as wedding parties. We would like to be able to keep this going to bring in extra money. The main theme of the Centre will be to offer a service to other community groups who wish to meet, either on a social basis or to carry out business-related activities. We currently host the Women's Planning Meetings for Women's Information Day (WID) and have acted as host for the WID by using Shaftesbury Recreation Centre. We felt that it would be much more suitable to be able to use our own premises for such functions, which can bring in quite large amounts of income.

Community Launderette

The Hot Iron is one project which we have been working on since 1990. Many funding applications were made for the project, and just within the past few months we have received word of substantial commitment to the project from several bodies. The aim is to provide a service to the local community, to the student and short-stay population, and to passing trade. The launderette will specialize in several options at competitive prices, such as ironing, delivery, and hand washing. We also hope to create at least six jobs. We have carried out a survey based on a sample of 200 people which has determined the need for the project in general. An analysis of results is still to be carried out to establish the need for each of the options, as mentioned above. This is the second survey to be carried out on the project, the first of which was done in 1989. We felt that an update was necessary to reinforce any research carried out before.

Continental Restaurant

In order to raise the quality of the Lower Ormeau Road, we decided that a high-class restaurant is necessary, which will encourage more visitors to the area. This attempt to go upmarket will coincide with the general redevelopment of the whole area.

Repair/Alterations Workshop

Since 1989, we have been holding craft and needlework classes, which were tutored by a lecturer from Rupert Stanley College. Unfortunately, due to a lack of resources, facilities and manpower to organize the classes, we were unable to start them off again when the new term began in September 1992, much to our disappointment and that of the ladies who attended. All of them, totalling approximately ten (numbers varied occasionally), had learned how to make clothes for their families, how to make alterations, and along with general crafts, how to create beautiful items for their homes. They all took a lot of pride in their work and we were amazed at what they were able to produce.

Over those four years, the ladies have become very skilled at needlecraft work, which is very much in demand. In many instances, it is currently difficult to find a local dressmaker. Having a number of dressmakers, we will be able to meet any demand. It is hoped, though, that more skills will develop and new students will attend the classes, once we start them again. The proposed workshop will have the added advantage of being well-advertised.

What really excites us is the thought of having all five amenities under one roof. Imagine being a visitor: you could come in with your washing and whilst it was being done, along with the ironing and any repairs you might need, you could be having a good meal. After that you might go along to the conference room to meet with others, and perhaps you'd be off down by the river to take a stroll before you went to bed. Then again, that might even be in the same building if you were staying at the hostel.

All my life I've been very interested in getting things together. I mean *really* together, so that one thing sparks off another and there's a relationship between each and every part. Both our main projects that we are currently working on, the gasworks development and the Five Acorns, have this characteristic. To me, that is what gives them hope and will make them work. That, and the fact that they're so needed.

∞

NINE

A Letter to My Grandchildren

I end this book with a message to my grandchildren, for they are the ones that will be building their lives when mine has ended. My own children are doing that right now. They're still around and living close by, except of course for Gary.

My dear family,
Maybe just at this moment you're looking at me and the busy life I lead, saying to yourselves, 'She's not wise.' I could understand if that was the case, because it must look like a lot of hard work and very little progress. But I think you will appreciate what I'm trying to do when you're older and can see that people who work in the community, giving so much of their time, are doing it because they believe in it. Whole systems are wrong, right under our noses, and we are trying to change things so that it is fairer for all those who follow on, including you.

I could have agreed to move away from the Ormeau Road district, as you know, but I chose to stay because I love it. There are good people living here, homely people on both sides, who would be the first to offer help if anything went wrong. These are the ones I feel for, and there's no doubt they deserve better than they get.

It's a hope of mine that some of you will want to carry on my work, but I'd never expect it of you as I believe in free choice and independence. What is more important, and what I would like to think all my children possessed, is a gift for caring for our fellow human beings. You've heard people say, 'You've no nature in you.' That means you don't care. I'd want you all to have nature for people, more than anything else.

To my many grandchildren, those already born and those to come:

Never do something because you think it is the 'right' thing to do. Do it because you love it. I'd be delighted if any of you read my life story and got interested in community work, but it isn't easy. You find yourself constantly struggling to get someone interested in a scheme, searching around for money to set something up. Then, at last, the jigsaw falls into place a wee bit at a time and one day, you can hardly believe it, all the bits are in place and it's finished. So it is rewarding, but it will have taken an awful long time. You need to love doing it to keep going.

There are a few more things I've taken to heart and would like to pass on. No matter what work you do, I believe they apply.

Just recently, a few people have suggested that I should go in for some higher education so that I have more knowledge and know-how. This idea has certainly never appealed to me before, but I'm thinking about it. Now that we are about to expand into the Five Acorns scheme and the gasworks development I'm sure to be meeting loads of professional people and I'll need to be able to have my say. Having said that, I might be able to tell them a thing or two because I'm practical and on the spot. What I never ever want to learn, and it's something a lot of educated people do only too well, is how to talk down to ordinary women. I've heard some community workers saying things like: 'These are my women here, this is my woman there.' You'd think they were cows they were talking about. More often than not, they are hard-working women who don't need ordering about. You have to meet them at their level because they are people in their own right, not 'ours'. They are individuals who deserve respect and a chance to do their own thing. I don't believe in controlling people. That way, you get the worst out of them and belittle them, which you must never do. If getting more education made me forget this, I'm far better off without it.

So, treat people right no matter what their background and value them because they are human beings, the same as you. That goes for the old, too, who often get set aside. We have a young community in the Ormeau Road, but we also have a lot of elderly people in the area who have just given up. After a certain age, life seems to have stopped for them. It certainly shouldn't be like that. In fact, it's ridiculous when you think that older people have more wisdom and experience than the young and could contribute a great deal.

Even when I was a young woman I always got a lot out of talking with older people. Mrs Poots lived next door to me when I was a girl. She died at ninety-two, after having it awful hard all her life. She told me she had to get up at six o'clock every morning to get to work and remembered running past the big clock in the High Street in her bare feet when she was hardly more than a child. Millworkers like her were paid very little, but they were glad to get it because the poor house was just behind the hospital. It was a place people dreaded having to go. Mrs Poots filled me in with a lot of history, as well as making me appreciate that wee bit extra that we have today.

When you're young, it's easy to think the world is your oyster, with such a lot around you and everything there for the taking. Then when you can't get hold of much, either through unemployment or poverty, you become very discontented. Too often it's only when you get older that you really value what you have, including the free things like friendship, sunshine and flowers.

Another thing I'd like you to think about is how to use power. When you live in Northern Ireland you'd have to be blind not to see how much power is misused by those who have it. There is an expression: 'If you put a beggar on horseback it'll ride to hell', which is so true of the men who have power in this country. Women don't have much power, even today, but things are changing slowly. Now there are a whole lot of confident young women going through college and university who could gain some. They should know how easily power can go to a person's head. My own view is that women are often more sensible than men. If we could get it through to them to use their power in the right way, we could bring about wonders.

But none of these things can you do if you have hate in your heart. My children, your parents, had a terrible lot to put up with when Gary was murdered. They could so easily have destroyed themselves from within if they had allowed hate to take over. It has taken years for all of us to be able to stand back, and it's only just now that I can think about it and say: we have an awful habit of condemning people before we look at the reason for them doing things. We should be asking ourselves, 'What makes this sort of thing happen?' Instead, we act so high and mighty or feel so distressed that we don't really look at it. The result is, we don't tackle what causes such violence.

Perhaps some of what lies behind it is that we don't like things that are different from ourselves. If we are Catholic we don't like Protestants and vice versa. The young often have no interest in older people and don't like them, and the older people disapprove of the young. I remember going to Docklands, in London, and meeting some wonderful, young Bangladeshi women who were learning to be modern and more independent of their men. There was a lot of racial tension around and they weren't liked for the colour of their skins. Yet people spend a lot of money trying to get brown, or they did before the skin cancer scare. How then can they look down on the ones who are brown already? Even before some white people felt threatened economically, there was that rift between coloured and white.

The truth is, if things go wrong people tend to blame somebody else. It'll be coloured people or society or the Government, anything so long as it isn't themselves. When you have a problem, whether it is at work or in the home, I think you have to take time to study it honestly, over and over again, until you find out what is at the root of it. That way it's not half as bad and if it's curable, you can cure it.

All these are serious thoughts that need considering, but there's another side of life which I have found equally important. That is, having a lot of cheek. As you will all know, I have never been without this one characteristic and owe a lot of great happenings in my life to it. One of the best things it did for me was getting me really noticed on radio for the first time.

I haven't mentioned it, but myself and one or two other women used to do short bits on the subject of poverty on Downtown Radio at the end of the record sessions. One day we were being asked the usual questions about where money would come from to help the poor. I knew that upstairs in the recording studio nobody would be censoring the programme. Probably they'd all have gone out thinking 'Just a couple of working women who don't make sense.' So then and there I made the suggestion that the Government should cut down on nuclear arms. I put it very forcefully, and added that it would give every family in Britain an extra £30 a week if they did. The next moment all the telephone lines were blasting with people that agreed, and the studio operators were jumping back up the stairs. It took them some time to get control of the situation, and we women hardly had a dry knicker between us we were laughing so much. We got the sack, but it was worth it. So don't be forgetting the cheek!

What I want to see before I finally pack up is the Ormeau Road and the five communities around it all coming to life and working together. I would like to think of all my grandchildren, and everybody else's too, enjoying that. The way I look at it, it's a small area we live in but the problems here are not that different from those in all the inner-cities of Ireland, England, Scotland and Wales. We have the ideas to help put things right and we have made the plans. If we can become a model of improvement for others to follow we will, even if it takes Janice having to wheel me around in my wheelchair to persuade people to listen and to act.

What a challenge there is right in front of us. If God spares me to do the work I so badly want to do, there will be another book written I'm sure.